Girl
net

Girl
net

The Girls' Guide to the Internet and More!

SARRA MANNING
Illustrated by Phil Corbett

The Chicken House
AN EGMONT JOINT VENTURE

Dedicated to my dad who went from newbie to net head in a matter of minutes and can always be relied upon for instant 'puter advice and hard-disk hand-holding. Thanks Pops.

© The Chicken House 2001
Text © Sarra Manning 2001
Illustrations © Phil Corbett 2001

First published in Great Britain in 2001
The Chicken House
2 Palmer Street
Frome
Somerset BA11 1DF
United Kingdom

Cover and text design by Rob Biddulph and Alison Withey.
Printed and bound in Great Britain.

British Library Cataloguing in Publication data available.
Library of Congress Cataloging in Publication Data available.

ISBN 1-903434-15 7

Contents

Introduction

A whole book on the internet! You're probably standing there thinking one of three things:

1. Let me at the mouse, I can't wait to start clicking.
2. The world wide web is an icky, frightening place and if I touch any stray buttons trying to get on the internet I'm likely to either get a headache or break my computer.
3. I already know how to send e-mails and use the internet - so who the heck needs a whole book on the subject?

All good responses. But **Girl Net** is not like any other computer book you've ever tried to read before - and ended up nodding off to dreamville instead.

Easy to understand

For starters, **Girl Net** isn't written in strange, techie-speak. It's easy to understand and if there are any 'puter-related words that make you go, "Huh?" a quick flick to our net glossary at the back of the book will have you unwrinkling that frown.

And **Girl Net** doesn't assume that you know nothing about the web or loads about it. If you barely know how to turn on a computer you'll find **Girl Net** to be a gentle, hand-holding trip in to the world wide web. We'll give you loads of sound, easy to understand advice about getting connected to the internet, sending e-mails and even stuff that you never imagined you'd be able to do - like making your own website or even transferring cool little net gizmos from the net on to your computer, so it can do whizzy things like play music and speak to you. Our book, as well as being a net guide, is also a story about two girls called Lotty and Grace. And as Lotty and Grace learn about the web, so do you.

Wow!

But if you are a bit of a net head, **Girl Net** will also open your eyes to a whole load of web-related goodness that you didn't know existed. That could be everything from cool sites and cunning tips on how to search the net in super-fast time, new things to do with e-mails instead of just writing to your mates to tell them that you're bored and pointers on cool stuff you can download. And while you might not need to know about all the new cyber diskoveries our net girls Lotty and Grace are making, you might want to read their e-mails to find out all their gossip.

And if you're somewhere in between net newbie and net head, then **Girl Net** will give you the confidence to try out new stuff on the net and even pretty up your computer by showing you how to take pics and sounds from the web and stick them on your desktop.

You can use **Girl Net** alongside your computer to look up stuff as you're actually doing it. Or you can just curl up in a comfy chair with a side helping of chocolate and read **Girl Net** in one sitting. Then maybe next time you are in front of a 'puter you'll have a better understanding of how this thing called the internet actually works.

Techie stuff and gossip

You might also be wondering why this book is called **Girl Net** when boys are in on this web thing too. Well, **Girl Net** is written by a girl for girls so you can take the girl-shaped world you live in and make it more net-friendly. **Girl Net** isn't just about being able to do techie stuff - it's about using the web to do all the things you like to do anyway whether it's keeping in touch with your mates, making new friends, flirting with boys or just catching up with gossip.

But more importantly **Girl Net is an attitude**. Ignore all those oldsters who reckon computers are for boys (and sadly there are a few of them still about) and make yourself a part of the web. It doesn't matter how you do it. It could be as simple as getting an e-mail account or going into a chat-room. Or it could even be about really putting your mark on to the internet by creating your own website or starting your own e-mail newsgroup. And if you're feeling a bit mad, you could even use the internet to score an A in your history project - but there are way more exciting things to do on the world wide web than to use it to do your homework! **Girl Net** will help you find out what they are.

So, dive into this book, find a computer and get online where a whole new world awaits you.

And if you're still looking at this book in total disgust, 'cause you either hate all things computer-related or are already so down with technology that you own your own dot.com start up, here's some other stuff you can do with this book.

Ten alternative uses for Girl Net:

1 A drinks coaster
Perfect for placing under a steaming mug of hot choccy.

2 Hamster cage lining
Maybe Fluffy will appreciate the softness of **Girl Net**'s pages while he's having a snooze.

3 Modern Art
Girl Net's cover is bright and cheerful - so why not put it in a nice frame and hang it on your wall?

4 A bartering tool
Swap **Girl Net** for nail varnish, chocolate or a small, cuddly toy.

5 Table straightening device
Maybe your desk is wobbly. Shoving **Girl Net** under one of its legs will give you a sturdy surface to work on. Hurrah!

6 Boy magnet
In love with a net boy? Whip out **Girl Net** whenever he's in the area and strike up a conversation about this new-fangled net thingy.

7 Money maker
If your mates need computer advice you could rent them this book, saving them from having to buy a copy and making yourself some cash at the same time.

8 **A weapon**

Girl Net is a perfect missile for throwing at annoying little siblings who keep obscuring your view of the telly.

9 **A portable fan**

If the summer heat is making you break out in a sweat, **Girl Net** can be fanned in front of your face to create a delightful breeze.

10 **If your 'rents forget to go to the supermarket and buy toilet roll you could rip out the pages of this book and sell them at a sheet a time, making even more dosh!**

However, **Girl Net** really is a non-scary, girl's guide to kicking it in cyber land. Oh, go on ... give it a try!

① Welcome to the wonderful web world!

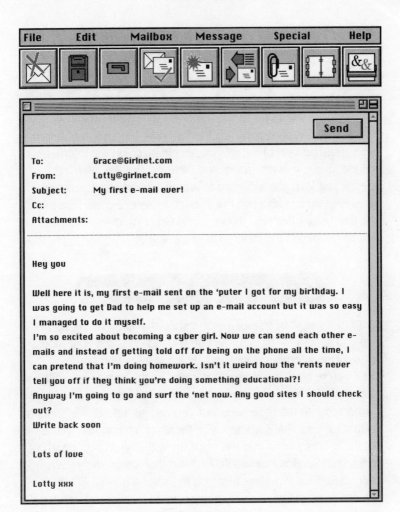

It used to be that computers were big old things that took up a whole room and needed lots of boffin types in white coats with letters after their names to be able to use one. Not anymore. You've probably got a computer at home and you definitely get to use one at school. You can do loads of things with a computer from writing poetry to designing a state-of-the-art history project complete with illustrations but it's once you go online (connect to the internet) that things get really fun-shaped.

So what is the internet?

The internet is simply a whole bunch of computers able to connect to other computers all around the world. This means that if someone wants to place their work on the world wide web (which is yet another name for the internet), then it's available to everyone. The kind of things that people place on the internet include music, movies, books and pictures. But the internet doesn't just give you a chance to snoop around other people's websites, you can also use the internet to send e-mails (like the one that Lotty's just sent to her friend Grace) and you can even chat to people on the other side of the world.

How to get on the internet

If you're using your school 'puter it should already be set up to give you access to the web. All you have to do is roll your mouse on to a little internet symbol and click and away you go.
But if you're on a brand new 'puter you might have to get a little bit technical. There are usually a couple of cables that need to be connected into the right holes but you can get one of the 'rents to do that for you, that's what they're there for after all (the 'rents not the cables!) What you will need to do though is sign up with an Internet Service Provider (ISP). Even this is incredibly easy. Internet Service Providers give you the software (on a CD that you put into your 'puter) and all you have to do is follow four or five simple instructions that come up on your 'puter screen.

They'll look something like this:

You can get your mitts on one of these clever little CDs from a ton of different places. Lots of shops like WH Smiths, HMV and Topshop give away internet

```
┌─────────────────────────────────┐ ■
│ Welcome to girl.com             │
│ Please follow these simple instructions │
│ Name     ┌──────────────────┐   │
│          └──────────────────┘   │
│ Password ┌──────────────────┐   │
│          └──────────────────┘   │
│ Location ┌──────────────────┐   │
│          └──────────────────┘   │
│  ┌────────┐  ┌──────────────┐   │
│  │  Send  │  │   Continue   │   │
│  └────────┘  └──────────────┘   │
└─────────────────────────────────┘
```

access CDs (and they're free) or you may even find one stuck to the front of a magazine, posted through your letter box or even given away at your local cinema. As well as getting you onto the internet, they'll also offer you webspace so you can make your own website (but we'll talk about that later) and a number of free e-mail addresses. And if you start off with an ISP and don't like 'em you can always put in another CD and choose an ISP that you do like.

Now this all might sound like a lot to take in but it's completely non-scary. If you do have trouble following the instructions there will be a helpline number that you can ring up (remember to get 'rental permission because it may be a premium rate service) and a techie type on the other end of the phone will take you through the procedure step-by-step. **But, hey, you're a net girl, you'll do fine.**

You've got mail

Congratulations 'cause you now have all you need to get on the net and start surfing. But before you do that, let's do the e-mail thing 'cause that's probably what you'll use the net for most. E-mail is electronic mail that you write on your 'puter and then send it to someone else's puter. Just like a letter but way, way more sophisticated than that!

The first thing you need to do is invent an e-mail address. Your ISP will provide the second bit of the address (that's the bit after the @) but you can have loads of fun thinking up a cool net name for yourself. Of course, you could just use your real name but you could also get creative.

Fr'instance you could be maltesermuncher@yourISP.com or girlinahurry@yourISP.com or even thecoolestgirlintheworld@yourISP.com.

The possibilities are endless. And because most ISPs give you five

Text Toolbar

File - This menu will help you send, receive and create new e-mails.
Edit - Use this menu to fiddle around with the text, change stuff and check spellings.
Mailbox - Use this menu to open mailboxes.

Message - Use this menu to create, delete and resend e-mails.
Special - Lots of fancy tricks here like address books and ways to organise your e-mails to make your life easier.
Help - Where to go when you're having problems.

Button Toolbar
Click on these buttons and this is what will happen

Delete - this will bin any unwanted messages.

Outbox - This is the mail folder that stores all the messages you sent.

Inbox - And this is the mail folder that stores all the messages you've received.

Check mail - This will tell you if you have new mail.

New message - This will give you a bank e-mail page to start writing on.

Forward - This lets you send the e-mail you've just received on to someone else.

Attachments - This will start the process of attaching a document, pic or photo onto your e-mail.

Address book - This is how to open the address book where you can store all your e-mail addresses.

Print - This will print your e-mails for you.

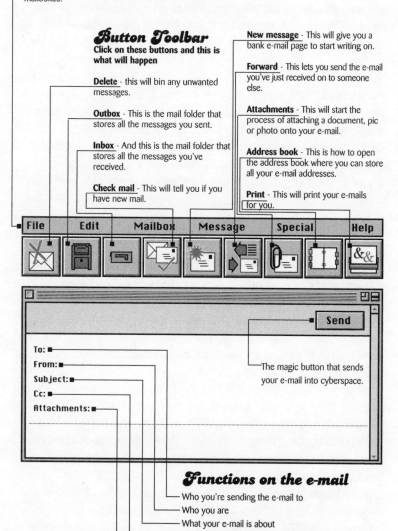

| File | Edit | Mailbox | Message | Special | Help |

Send

The magic button that sends your e-mail into cyberspace.

To: ■
From: ■
Subject: ■
Cc: ■
Attachments: ■

Functions on the e-mail

Who you're sending the e-mail to
Who you are
What your e-mail is about
Anyone else you want to send the e-mail to
Any files you're sending with the e-mail

different e-mail accounts (for no charge) you can even use different addresses for different people. You could have one address that you only give to your best mate, another address for receiving newsletters and another address for school friends. It's entirely up to you.

Sending e-mails is also easy. It's best to write your e-mails off-line (so you can save on the phone bill) and go online just to send them.

At the top of your blank e-mail page there'll be a toolbar which is a line of instruction buttons and below that will be a space to write the e-mail address you're mailing to. You don't even have to put in your own address as the ISP will do that for you automatically. Then you write down what you want to say, press 'send' and off your e-mail goes to land in your mate's mailbox faster than it took you to read this sentence.

Your address book

Sometimes e-mail addresses can be tricky little things to remember with loads of dashes and dots. But, once again, some techie bods have devised a clever way of memorising e-mail addresses so you don't have to.

All e-mail software has a feature called an address book which stores e-mail addresses for you. The software can vary depending on what e-mail programme you use but it shouldn't be very difficult to work out what to do. Usually all you need to do is to open the e-mail, then go to the toolbar and click on the 'tool' button to find an instruction that will say something like "add to contacts". You click on that and then you never have to type in the e-mail address ever again. Instead you go to the address book button on your toolbar, click on it and find the address you need. **The other nifty thing about the address book is that it lets you give nicknames to your list of addresses.** So, say, you know two people called Emma, the address book will let you change their names to Emma Blonde and Emma Brown so you don't get confused. But it's worth remembering that the nickname will appear on the e-mail that you send to them so if you don't like them very much try to resist the temptation to give them a rude nickname otherwise you might find yourself on the receiving end of a stroppy e-mail!

Internet e-mail accounts

Although you need an ISP to get online to send e-mails, you don't have to use the ISP's e-mail system. Instead you can send e-mails via a website. Lots of websites let you use their e-mail facilities and it costs now't, nothing, no pounds, nada.

Instead of only being able to send and receive e-mails from your own 'puter, web-based e-mails mean you can check and send mail from any 'puter set up for internet access. Just think, you can e-mail your American pen-pal while you're at school or tell your best mate that you've just bumped into her crush object snogging another girl from an internet café.

There are lots of web-based e-mail services to choose from. Big sites like www.yahoo.com or www.microsoft.com all have their own e-mail facilities with lots of added bits of netty goodness. There are also websites that specialise only in e-mails and will let you have the most wiggy addresses ever.

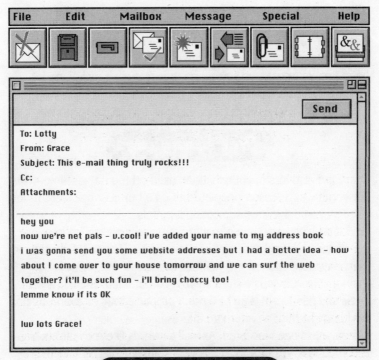

The Write Stuff

As you can probably tell from Grace's e-mail, things like punctuation and capital letters don't really matter online. The thing about e-mail is that it lets you write just how you talk. And if you're like most people, that means you don't worry too much about stuff like capital letters and punctuation and correct grammar when you're nattering to your mates.

A lot of e-mails that get sent are only a couple of lines long anyway and life's way too short to worry about whether you should put in commas when all you want to do is remind your friend what cinema you're meant to be meeting outside on Saturday.

Then again it's not worth losing any sleep if you're an English whizz and you feel weird about losing capital letters. The great thing about the 'net is that there are no rules. Everyone does pretty much what they feel like.

Besides if you do have to write an e-mail to someone adult-shaped like a teacher or a grandparent (yup, grand'rents have been known to get web savvy and there's even a nickname for them, silver surfers!) it's probably not a good idea to show off your cool net lingo. They're too old fashioned to really appreciate it.

Net Language

There are also lots of abbreviations used on the net and in e-mail. For some weird reason people don't go a bundle on vowels. If you get a message that says something like, "pls hlp! stk on h/w. wot pg?" it doesn't mean one of your friends has spilt orange juice on her 'puter keyboard again. What it means is, "Help me! I'm stuck on our homework and can't remember what page I'm meant to be memorising." **Obviously she's so wigged out about the homework crisis she hasn't got time to write a proper e-mail or even vowels.** And to make things even more interesting, a whole new net language has been invented. As well as words like "newbie" (which is someone who's new to all this web stuff) and "lurker", there are little symbols people use to describe themselves and the way they're feeling. These are called emoticons and can range from <g> which means the person you're mailing or chatting to has just grinned, to :-) (try looking at it sideways!) which is a smiley face. There are literally squillions of these and the last chapter of this book has most of them listed so you will never know a moment of confusion on your journey around the www.

② The internet and how to use it

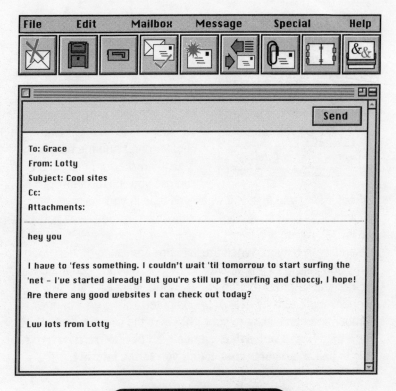

| File | Edit | Mailbox | Message | Special | Help |

Send

To: Grace
From: Lotty
Subject: Cool sites
Cc:
Attachments:

hey you

I have to 'fess something. I couldn't wait 'til tomorrow to start surfing the 'net - I've started already! But you're still up for surfing and choccy, I hope! Are there any good websites I can check out today?

Luv lots from Lotty

Caught in the net

So you now know how to get online and you know how to send e-mails but what do you do once you're connected? How do you find different sites? And how do you get from one site to another? Well, here comes the techie bit so read on and all will be revealed...

To get on the internet you simply click or double click your mouse on a little internet symbol that should appear on your 'puter's desktop (the desktop is simply another way to describe the screen of symbols that comes up once you've started your 'puter.)

Once you've clicked on it a little box will come up. It'll look something like this:

Select the service you want to connect to, and then enter your user name and password

Connect to   Your ISP.com

User name   Net Girl

Password   apple

☐ Save password
☐ Connect automatically

Connect   **Cancel**

These settings will be set when you first chose your ISP (see chapter one.) And the password is just to make sure that no one can use your ISP account without asking you first. But when you type in your password it will appear as little stars. So if your password is mouse, all you'll see is ****. Again, this is just to make sure that no one's pretending to be you. When the little box comes up though your name and password will already be filled in, all you need to do is click on the 'connect' button and then the strangest thing will happen. You'll actually hear your computer dialling up a phone number and connecting to your ISP. Once the call is accepted you'll then hear **a noise that sounds a bit like 'kerrrrrrrrrrrrrrr.! This is just your 'puter connecting you to the internet.**

You don't really need to know this to get on the internet but, hey, you might as well hear about it anyway and all knowledge is good. In your 'puter is a clever little device called a modem which lets your 'puter make phone calls to other 'puters. In this case it's calling up your ISP and saying , "Excuse me but my owner would like to go on the internet or send some e-mails, please can you connect her!" Sometimes instead of the "kerrrrrrrrrrr", you'll get an engaged tone of long beeps. This means that lots of people are trying to get on the internet all at the same time and your ISP is a bit too busy to connect you. Leave it a minute and click on the connect button again and before too long you'll be surfing to your heart's content!

You're probably all eager to start surfing but there's just a few more things you need to know about that will make your web wanders even more fun. The first of these is a web browser. Sounds complicated? Well, it isn't. Web browsers are the software that help you use the internet. You know how we said the internet was a whole bunch of 'puters connecting to each other? Well instead of your 'puter having to do all the hard work of connecting to a whole lot of other 'puters, the web browser does it all for you. Web pages are written in a complex computer code but a web browser automatically translates it for you so you get to see words and pictures and not lots of confusing symbols.

When you install your ISP software, the web browser is automatically downloaded onto your 'puter's internet function. The web browser will be called either Netscape Navigator or Microsoft Internet Explorer. It doesn't matter which one you use as they pretty much do the same thing.

Online at last

Finally your 'puter is set up, connected and ready to rumble. You've clicked the 'connect' button and the call has been accepted and after a minute of your computer whirring, up comes your homepage. The homepage is simply the first page that comes up when you first go online. Your ISP will automatically select their site as your homepage, hoping that you'll use their facilities such as e-mail and news services but you can easily change your homepage by going into your internet settings. It depends on your 'puter software so instead of explaining how to do it here the best thing is to either check your 'puter instructions or have a fiddle around with the toolbar.

Text Toolbar

File - This menu will help you move to different places on the net and print out webpages.

Edit - You can move text from webpages into normal word files and this menu will help you.

View - Lots of techie ways to change the look of your internet settings.

History - A list of different webpages you've been browsing.

Favourites - The menu that contains all the websites you've bookmarked (added to your favourites folder.)

Help - Where to go when you're stuck.

Button Toolbar
Click on these buttons and this is what will happen

Back - Go back to the last webpage you were on.

Forward - Go forward a page.

Stop - Stop the page that's currently downloading.

Refresh - If the webpage hasn't downloaded properly, the refresh (or reload) button will download it again.

Larger - Makes the page text and pictures bigger.

Smaller - Makes the page text and pictures weenier.

Search - A quick way to get to a search engine.

Home - How to get back to the page you started on.

Print - Print out the webpage.

Favourites - A quick way to get to your favourites folder.

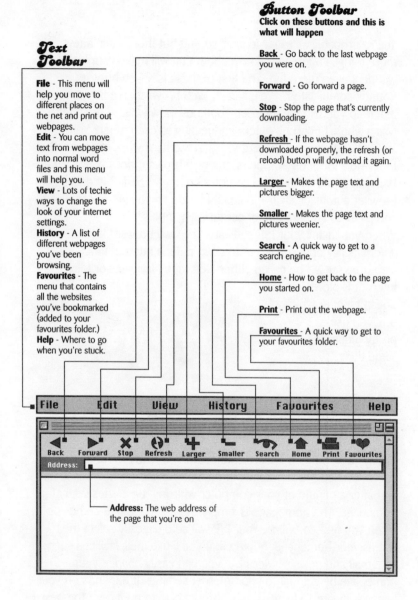

File   Edit   View   History   Favourites   Help

Back   Forward   Stop   Refresh   Larger   Smaller   Search   Home   Print   Favourites

Address:

Address: The web address of the page that you're on

To make matters easier this is what you can expect a webpage to look like and this is **what all those weirdy buttons actually do.**

So now you're on the internet with your homepage set up, where do you go? Like there's a whole world wide web out there so how do you sort out the good sites from the sucky sites?

Just looking

There are many ways to move round the web. If you already have a web address that you want to investigate, all you need to do is move your cursor (that little vertical line that moves around the page when you touch your mouse) up to the little white box just under your toolbar. It will already have the web address of your homepage typed in and to get rid of it, you move your cursor onto the web address, click it once and the whole line will become highlighted. Then you just type in the address you want to go to and press your 'return' key and then 1, 2, 3, (and a few more whirring noises from your 'puter) and you're there. Remember that all web addresses start with 'www' which stands for (and you already know this!) world wide web. Once the new page comes up, the start of the address will have "http://" miraculously added. This stands for something incredibly techie called Hypertext Transport Protocol which you really do not need to know about. **It's just a little message to your 'puter.**

Finding **cool websites** isn't that difficult. Just take a good look around your world. Fr'instance there'll be website addresses on soft drink cans, on adverts, at the end of television programmes and even on cereal packets. And you could just visit these sites (especially if you really like cereal!) but you'd be missing out on a ton of cool cyber experiences.

The next way to find sites is by using a little guesswork and a little common sense. You already know that all website addresses begin with "www" but they also usually end in "com" (for American or big UK sites) or "co.uk" (which means that the site is British.) It's just the bit in the middle that you need to fill in. So if you wanted to go to the Coca Cola site, it's a pretty safe guess that the address would be www.cocacola.com and that the official site for Dawsons Creek would be www.dawsonscreek.com. You usually separate the different sections of the address with a full stop or a slash. Not all sites are easy to find or so easy to type in. There may be lots of little sections that combine to make an address and you might have to use slashes and underscores and other fiddly keys that you've never used before.

But life's too short to spend serious surfing time trying out different addresses to see if they're actually websites and you'll be pleased to know that once again some clever 'puter boffins have already been on the case!

I still haven't found what I'm looking for

Search engines are a net girl's best friend. And they have absolutely nothing to do with actual engines. What they do though is help people to find what they're looking for on the web.

There are stacks of search engines to choose from. Far too many to list but some that you might want to try out include:

> **www.yahoo.com or www.yahoo.co.uk**
> **www.altavista.com**
> **www.hotbot.com**
> **www.lycos.com**
> **www.excite.com or www.excite.co.uk**

Most search engines work in the same way. There's a little box where you type in what you're looking for and then click on the "search" button which should be located very near the box. And then, as if by magic but actually by something called Boolean maths, the search engine will find what you're looking for and come up with a cheery message that says, **"There are 23,795 web matches for cute boys"** and you'll run screaming from your 'puter and have to have a lie-down in a dark room.

The trick is to narrow down your search. So instead of just looking for cute boys, you could actually type in the name of a boy you're looking for. And if you put the name into speechmarks, the search will only give you websites where those words appear. Fr'instance if you type in the name "Backstreet Boys", the search engine will supply you with a list of sites about the Backstreet Boys instead of sites about the Backstreet Boys plus a whole ton of other sites about backstreets and boys. This is called a keyword search.

Another way to search is to use the categories provided on the search site's homepage. If you go to Yahoo, you'll see headings like "Entertainment", "News And Media" and "Recreation And Sports". If you click on a heading you'll then be sent to another section and given some more choices to click on until after a few more clicks you'll be able to find what you were looking for.

But the weird thing about surfing is that sometimes the sites you find along the way can be more exciting and fun than the site you were trying to find.

Your bestest sites ever

During your surfing you'll stumble upon many weird and
wonderful sites that you'll want to visit again and again. But,
ooops, you've forgotten what the web address is! Don't you just
hate it when that happens? It doesn't have to be a problem
though.

If you want to add a site to your 'puter's memory, just go to the
"favourites" section of your toolbar, click and hold down with your
mouse and then scroll down to the option that reads "Add page to
your favourites folder" and click on it. The page is then saved for
ever and ever. Easy much!

③ Sites for sore eyes

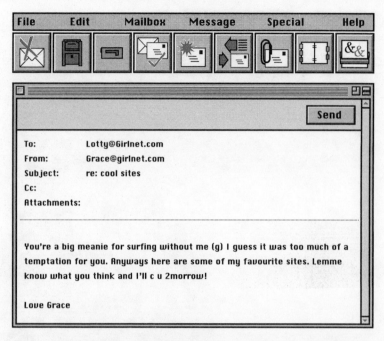

| File | Edit | Mailbox | Message | Special | Help |

Send

To: Lotty@Girlnet.com
From: Grace@girlnet.com
Subject: re: cool sites
Cc:
Attachments:

You're a big meanie for surfing without me (g) I guess it was too much of a temptation for you. Anyways here are some of my favourite sites. Lemme know what you think and I'll c u 2morrow!

Love Grace

There's a world wide web waiting for you out there, but to ease you in gently here are some cool sites to check out while you're finding your way around:

www.dawsonscreek.co.uk

This is the official site for the American telly programme about love-crazed high school students. It has all the stuff that you'd expect to find, like episode summaries and actor profiles, but it also has some unique bits of net goodness (also called "killer apps") that you won't find anywhere else. First check out Dawson's Desktop which lets you sneak around Dawson Leary's home 'puter and read his online diary and his e-mails from other characters in the show. Then check out some of Dawson's Favourite Websites and you'll find homepages for the other characters. You can also sign up for a weekly e-mail that will keep you informed of all the goings-on in Capeside.

www.bloomsbury.com/harry potter

This is the official UK site for the micro wizard (the US site can be found at www.scholastic.com/harry potter) and there's more to it than just a place to buy books and read an interview with Harry Potter creator JK Rowling. Depending on whether you're a witch or a wizard or even a muggle you can get to different areas of the site, take part in competitions and even play a virtual game of Quidditch, as well as testing your Harry trivia knowledge in quizzes and other magical malarkey.

www.barbie.com

Now you might think you outgrew playing with Barbies aeons ago but the plastic princess site is worth checking out. As well as letting you meet Barbie and her mates (OK you can skip that bit if you want) there's a feature that lets you design your own Barbie doll. You can choose different skin tones, eye colour, hair shades and even the exact redness of Barbie's lips, before getting to kit her out in a variety of eye-catching outfits. At the end of your creative session there is an option to actually buy your own unique Barbie, but unless you really haven't given up playing with dollies and your 'rents are quite happy to let you loose on the net with their credit card, you might have to forgo this treat.

www.smartgirl.com

This site wants to know what you think about everything. You can write reviews on everything from films to your favourite magazine, get advice, read your horoscope and, best of all, check out if the boy of your dreams is really meant for you with Smartgirl's crush barometer.

www.sanrio.com

Welcome to Hello Kitty's virtual world. This is where the mouthless cat hangs out with her mates Keroppi, Little Twin Stars and other cutesome 'toons. Even though you can't buy any of the stuff on this site unless you're a US resident, you can send your friends Hello Kitty e-cards (we'll talk about 'em later) and have some serious fun with the Hello Kitty story-making kit. Under subjects like "Hello Kitty Throws A Party" you get to supply a long list of words, before clicking on a button and reading your very own Hello Kitty short story. The trick is to get as weird with your word choices as you possibly can and then e-mail your friends the sometimes startling results. A good way to waste hours of valuable homework time.

www.gurlpages.com

Gurlpages is a completely cool US site that provides a girl-shaped place to get to grips with the internet. After registering you can then send e-mail from your own gurlpages e-mail account (remember with internet based e-mail accounts you can send and receive e-mails from any computer set up for internet access). Gurlpages also provides you with webspace to make your own website and stress-free help and instructions too. If you don't feel ready for that, check out some of the other gurlpagers' websites - there are hundred and hundreds of them here from Buffy The Vampire Slayer fan-sites to eco-warrior homepages. Gurlpages also has its own site with virtual palm-reading, makeovers and chat-rooms. You can spend hours here!

www.ultranet.com/~adjm/java/bsnap/bubblesnap.shtml

You know how satisfying it is to pop bubblewrap? Well, if you mosey on down to this website you can do it virtually, just by clicking your mouse on the little circles. Each successful click even comes with its own popping sound.

www.joecartoon.com

This is a joke and novelty site with lots of interactive bits and bobs for you to try out. Probably two of the most famous applications here are "frog in a blender" and "fish in a blender" which lets you purée harmless creatures as a way of getting rid of any pent-up anger you might have. Just don't try it at home, OK?

www.nike.com

This is the official site of our favourite trainer makers and is the last word in high-tech net trickery. You might find it a little boy-oriented, what with all the talk of footie, but there are some amazing games to be found here as well as the very latest in net graphics.

www.trouble.co.uk

This is Trouble TV's website so expect lots of programme information and interviews with Trouble presenters. But check out their fantastic Flash Boyfriend game. This is a cartoon that you control. You get to go on dates with Max, plus you get to choose what happens. So if he's getting on your nerves you can tell him to put a sock in it, or if he's being all cute and lovely you can snog him! Max will send you regular e-mails asking you to meet him on dates - but beware of Felix his tricky flatmate and Steph his evil ex-girlfriend.

.com

www.bbc.co.uk/eastenders

This is where the web meets Walford. Catch up with all the latest goings-on in Albert Square, chat to other 'Enders' fans - and even the stars of the soap - and get the chance to give Dot Cotton a makeover. And about time too!

www.benandjerry.co.uk

There's more to this website than simply ice cream, although you can read about that here if you're suffering from hunger pangs. As well as regular competitions (you could even get the chance to create your own dream ice cream) there are screensavers, e-cards, a Girthometer and a very, very strange "Thumping Moo" game.

www.quizbox.com

Quizzes are usually the first thing most girls turn to in magazines, but when you do them on the net you don't have to spend five minutes working out your score. Not when technology can do it for you. Quizbox has a huge database of quizzes, with more added regularly - so now you can find out exactly what makes you tick.

www.yahooligans.com

We've already talked about Yahoo the search engine, now meet Yahooligans, the kid-friendly version. Instead of having to wade through lots of boring, oldster stuff about the stockmarket and computer software, Yahooligans takes a more fun approach to looking up stuff on the net, as well as having e-mail and chat features.

www.surfmonkey.com

If you get a bit scared at how big the web is and how many weird people and sites there are, then surf monkey's here to give you a helping hand. They have a cool, safe sites download that will automatically block out any icky web stuff you might stumble upon, plus the surf monkey club will give you access to games, interactive stories as well as all the usual chat and e-mail goodies you've come to expect.

www.missdorothy.com

Dot.com, geddit? Unlike a lot of sites, Miss Dorothy is a British site designed just for girls under the age of twelve. You can learn about the web along with Dorothy and read her online diary. There's even a chance to write your own reviews and stories to be posted on the site.

www.grrlgamer.com

Some people might reckon that computer games are for boys - but they'd be mighty wrong. Grrlgamer is a computer games site by and for girls and will have all the latest tips on new games as well as "cheats" (shortcuts and sneaky ways to complete the games) and "walkthroughs" (a step-by-step guide) for when you get stuck. You'll particularly dig the attitudey way this site is put together and the cute little 'toons of grrlgamers.

www.outpost-daria.com

This is a fan-site for the cynical cartoon girl, Daria. As well as an episode guide and news about the show, Outpost Daria also has screensavers and wallpaper you can download on to your computer, a huge database of fan fiction (Daria fans writing their own stories about the characters) and a gallery of fan art.

www.agirlsworld.com

Described as "where girls rule the web", agirlsworld.com is an online magazine written by girls from all over the world. Which means there's nothing to stop you from getting in on some of this web-ruling action too!

www.sparknotes.com

Stuck with your English homework and can't work out what the poem you're meant to be studying is actually about? Sparknotes is a great educational website which has study notes on just about every book you might ever have to write an essay about.

www.buffy.com

The Vampire Slayer's official site comes complete with spooky graphics and little clips from every single episode of Buffy. You can also check out the various demons and ghouls that have terrorized Sunnydale before Buffy kicked their butt and also read up on your favourite Buffy characters.

www.foxkids.com

The official website of Foxkids, this is a great place to look for internet games and lots of cartoon-related net goodies. There's a special girl-only part of this site called the girls channel which is also worth checking out.

www.ctw.org/stickerworld

Stickerworld is an online game where you get to trade, collect and display electronic stickers and even build a webpage using your stickers to decorate it. There are huge lists of different stickers for you to collect, but you also get the chance to design your very own unique stickers too.

www.girltech.com

This girl-kerpowered site aims to "create a world for the adventurous spirit" which is a fine way to describe the kind of chicas who'll like this site. Although girltech is girl-friendly it's a wuss-free zone and has tons of sports and games stuff as well as chat and a Quote Of The Day to inspire you even further.

www.doublecluck.com

Check out this website for the coolest publisher and the coolest books. Hopefully **Girl Net**'s guide into e-culture will be persuading you of this!

www.thesimpsons.com

The official site for everyone's favourite yellow cartoon family. There's all the things you might expect here, including an episode guide and character facts, but you can also sign up for a free internet service and an e-mail address that has thesimpsons.com as its domain name. Ay Carumba as Bart would say!

These sites will guarantee you a good time, but check out even more sites which are mentioned in the other chapters of **Girl Net** - and don't be afraid to do your own surfing!

④ More mail

And you thought e-mail was about sending letters...

We talked a lot about e-mails and how to send 'em in Chapter One and by now you're probably doing the "new message" and "send" thing like you were born to it. But if you weren't paying attention or got knocked on the head since then, remember these handy tips.

Top ten tips for e-mail happiness:

1 Always, always check that you've got the right e-mail address. If in doubt use the "check names" function on your toolbar, or if you're e-mailing someone new phone 'em up and ask for their e-mail address.

2 If your e-mail address is unrecognisable as you (e.g. leoswife@yourisp.com) and you're e-mailing someone for the first time, put your name in the subject heading so it reads Subject: from: Jane Pain.

3 DON'T USE ALL CAPITALS IN A MESSAGE 'CAUSE IT LOOKS LIKE YOU'RE SHOUTING AND IS VERY, VERY RUDE!

4 Don't flame someone (be rude or abusive) in an e-mail 'cause chances are they'll keep their e-mail and re-read it constantly and cry themselves to sleep thinking about how nasty you are.

5 When you joke around via the medium of e-mail it can be hard to tell if you're kidding. Always read through what you've written before you click on "send".

6 Keep 'em shortish. If you're sending a friend your English essay to copy (tut tut), it's better to send it as an attachment.

7 And while keeping 'em short is good, make sure they're readable. Yes, vowels and punctuation might be for oldsters bt u wnt ppl 2 ndrstnd wot u're tlkn' bout!

8 Keep your password private. Do you really want all your mates to be able to access your inbox?

9 Never send people really large attachments, especially if they're movie clips. Some ISPs won't accept really large files and they can have a grrrr-inducing habit of making people's 'puters crash.

10 And it's worth repeating, always check you've got the right address. You don't want to send that bitchy e-mail to the person you're bitching about, just 'cause her name was in your head when you were filling out the address. Think it can't happen? Think again!

Follow these little rules and you'll be the queen of the net. Now let's have some more fun with e-mails...

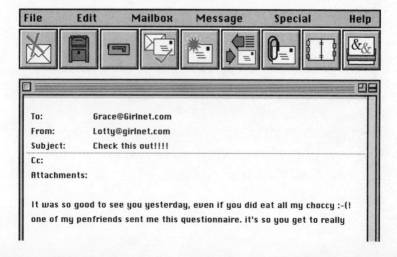

| File | Edit | Mailbox | Message | Special | Help |

To: Grace@Girlnet.com
From: Lotty@girlnet.com
Subject: Check this out!!!!
Cc:
Attachments:

It was so good to see you yesterday, even if you did eat all my choccy :-(!
one of my penfriends sent me this questionnaire. it's so you get to really

know your friends. i've filled it in and you have to reply to it, by pressing reply and then deleting all my answers and filling in your own ones. Then you send it back to me and try and send it to four other friends.

c ya!

E-MAIL QUESTIONNAIRE (make your answers as detailed as possible)

Name: Lotty

Age: 14

Lives: Manchester

Likes: Sleeping, finding new things to do with chocolate, nail varnish and my lovely new 'puter.

Dislikes: Jake Carter (he's such a pig!), getting moaned at by the 'rents, vegetables and homework.

Fave food: Chocolate (maltesers to be specific), thick-cut crisps and my mum's lasagne.

Worst food: Vegetables and tuna fish – it brings me out in a rash. Ewwww!

Fave drink: Diet coke (have to have three cans a day)

Worst drink: Weak tea (I hate it when it gets really milky)

Who's your crush: Josh Hartnett and Nick Giles from Year 13 (don't tell anyone that!)

Fave season: Summer, no school and two weeks in Greece.

Song in your head: Angels by Robbie Williams.

Tell us a secret: I can burp the alphabet.

If you could have a superpower what would it be: To be invisible for the day (so I could find out what Nick Giles really thinks about me.)

Fave book: The Lion, The Witch And The Wardobe (it might be a kids' book but I've read it about 50 times.)

Fave film: 10 Things I Hate About You

Fave place to live: In a lovely white villa in Paxos in Greece where we go for our holidays.

Fave website: www.gurlpages.com ('cause I've been there five times and there's still loads of stuff I haven't explored.)

What do you want to be when you grow up: A superhero.

Fave item of clothing: My jeans – they fit just right.

What's your favourite line of poetry: "Cats that swim in ink not sea really make me sick" (stoopid rhyme that my dad always recites when I'm in a mood).

Fave TV programme: The Simpsons

Mail Bonding

E-mail isn't just about writing to your mates when you've got a homework/boy/clothing/'rental unit (delete where applicable) crisis. Although it's pretty good for all those things too! E-mail is all about communicating - but that doesn't mean you have to stick to the standard "hey how are you?" rules. Remember that when it comes to this thing called the web there aren't any rules.

Once you've been net-connected for a couple of weeks and maybe registered with a few websites and e-mailed your mates a few times, you'll realise that your inbox (where your new e-mails are stored) is filling up. Now some of these e-mails will be bogstandard **"I hate Mandy she's such a cow and she eats her food really loudly"** type communications, but most of these e-mails will contain jokes, poems and even attached files that contain photos or little movie clips when you open them up.

It's probably not what the US military had in mind when they invented the internet (yup, they're the ones we have to thank!), but your e-mail inbox is a little window into you and your mates' world and if a little green alien managed to hack into your 'puter all he'd have to do is look at the e-mails you've sent and received to find out what you're into, what makes you laugh, what makes you hissy-fit and, hullo, just how many pictures of Pacey does one girl need?

So instead of using the e-mail just for urgent messages when your 'rents have put a lock on the phone, get creative. Being girl-shapes we've already mastered the art of being able to talk for hours about nothing (well if boys and nagging 'rents and why we need another bottle of glittery nail varnish can really be described as "nothing") so apply the same rules to e-mail. It's not just there for exchanging messages, it's there for whatever you want to do with it.

Send

To: Lotty@Girlnet.com
From: Grace@girlnet.com
Subject: One filled in questionnaire, present and correct.
Cc:
Attachments:

hey u! luv questionnaire thingy. am going to send it to everyone I know – all five of 'em!

E-MAIL QUESTIONNAIRE (make your answers as detailed as possible)
Name: Grace
Age: 14
Lives: Manchester
Likes: Annoying my big bro and my little bro.
Dislikes: Getting picked on by my brothers.
Fave food: Give me a family-sized bag of cheese 'n' onion crisps and I'll be your best friend.
Worst food: Liver, euwwwwww!
Fave drink: Peach juice.
Worst drink: Grapefruit juice.
Who's your crush: Any of the boys from Buffy The Vampire Slayer.
Fave season: Winter, I love curling up in front of the telly when it's all dark and cold outside.
Song in your head: Follow The Yellow Brick Road from The Wizard Of Oz.
Tell us a secret: I have five mouldy coffee mugs under my bed.
If you could have a superpower what would it be: A unique ability to accessorize.
Fave book: Violet And Claire by Francesca Lia Block.
Fave film: Romeo And Juliet.
Fave place to live: A windswept castle on a remote clifftop in Southern France.
Fave website: www.buffy.com – where I can get my vampire fix on a daily basis!
What do you want to be when you grow up: Either a vampire slayer or an astronaut. Maybe both.

Fave item of clothing: My Hello Kitty t-shirt that my aunt brought me
from Hong Kong.
What's your favourite line of poetry: "If I had a shiny gun, I could have
a world of fun/Speeding bullets through the brains of the folk who give me
pains." Claire, my big sis, taught me that one.
Fave TV programme: Buffy The Vampire Slayer, of course.

There are so many things that you can do via the medium of
e-mail that it would take a whole book just to describe them. Here
are just a fraction of them.

Top tens

Instead of waiting for the music charts to come out every Sunday
afternoon, you could compile your own list of favourite songs and
e-mail them to your mates. They don't even have to be songs -
you could do a Top Ten of favourite sandwich fillings, a Top Ten of
boys you have a secret crush on, or even a **Top Ten of stupid
sayings that your science teacher always comes out with.**

Round robins

Instead of writing short stories for the benefit of your English
mark, why not start a story then e-mail it to a friend to write the
next part? Then she'll e-mail another friend to write the third
instalment, who'll forward it on to another friend. Just make sure
that you don't get taken off the address list.

E-mail updates

If you have a favourite website that you go back to again and
again, look out for a place on the site to leave your e-mail address,
so you can be told when the site gets updated. If the site is
halfway decent it should subscribe to an updating service. And if it
doesn't, then e-mail the webmaster (the person who runs the site)

and suggest that they think about it!

E-mail newsletters and newsgroups

If you have a hobby or interest that takes up a lot of your free time, be it Dawson's Creek or gymnastics, check out a site called www.egroups.com .

E-groups acts as a library for lots of different mailing lists. There are lists for fan fiction and pottery-making - and even people who like Mexican tree frogs. (OK, I made the last one up!) Simply type what you're looking for in the search box and, lo and behold, a huge number of mailing lists will appear on your screen. It's dead easy to subscribe to and you can choose whether to get a copy of every e-mail that gets sent to your Dawson's Creek fan fiction list or instead get a daily digest. This way you can read what others think about your favourite stuff, send e-mails or fan fiction to the list yourself and best of all make some new e-pals. Alternatively you could become a "list mum" (someone who maintains and looks after an e-mail list) and start your very own mailing list. But beware - it might take you hours every day to wade through all the different e-mails from all the different lists you belong to.

Jokes

Heard a good joke and want to share it with the world? Bung it down on an e-mail and send it to your nearest and dearest. You can do the same thing with funny pictures that you find on the web - just download 'em, attach 'em to your e-mail and press send.

Return to Sender

It's an icky fact of life but when you get web active, you also fall prey to the "spammers" of this world. Spamming is when people or organizations post e-mails to thousands of different people. It's not difficult to figure out how to automatically send out shedloads of e-mails, but it's not nice so don't do it!

You don't have to be a spam victim though. So here are three cool ways to avoid the spammers or simply get rid of people you don't want mail from:

 If you have to leave an e-mail address on a message board or a newsgroup (eg. www.deja.com), actually write the words "no spam" into your address. Fr'instance, girl@nospamyourisp.com . This will foul up the spammer's evil plans, but if someone genuine wants to get in contact with you they should be clever enough to remove the "no spam" from your address.

 You may also get e-mail from large companies (or even small ones) promising you fantastic bargains on computer software or asking you to take part in dodgy, money-making chainletter schemes. You can either delete them and hope you don't get any more or you could actually reply to them, putting "REMOVE" or "UNSUBSCRIBE ME" in the subject box and leave the rest of the e-mail blank. Some of the spam you get sent will actually advise you to do this, but just hold up a sec. 'Cause sometimes the evil spammers want to know they've got active e-mail addresses and if you send an e-mail back to them, then they know that they've been successful in targeting you and they'll keep those e-mails a'coming. And often if you send the e-mail straight back to the spammers, you'll receive a failed message mail from your ISP telling you that there was an error in the address. These spammers are a tricky bunch.

 The best thing to do in the battle against spam is to use the "block sender" option which will keep that person's e-mail address on file and automatically delete any messages that they send you. Unfortunately a lot of e-mail applications don't have this feature but Hotmail does. So it might be an

idea to set up a Hotmail account and use that address if you
need to leave your e-mail details on a newsgroup or website.

If your friends persist in sending you chain e-mails about little
kiddies dying or bad luck falling on you and your family if you
don't send the e-mail on to ten other people, there's one more
thing you can do. Send all unwanted mail to
girlnetjunkbin@hotmail.com and we'll dump the pesky things for
you. But spam is a cyber fact of life and it's not worth losing sleep
over, so don't let it cramp your surfing style - **just be careful who
you give your e-mail address to.**

⑤ Chatter boxes

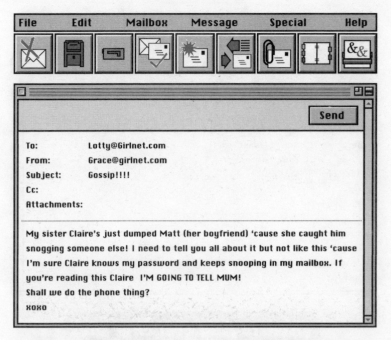

| File | Edit | Mailbox | Message | Special | Help |

Send

To: Lotty@Girlnet.com
From: Grace@girlnet.com
Subject: Gossip!!!!
Cc:
Attachments:

My sister Claire's just dumped Matt (her boyfriend) 'cause she caught him snogging someone else! I need to tell you all about it but not like this 'cause I'm sure Claire knows my password and keeps snooping in my mailbox. If you're reading this Claire I'M GOING TO TELL MUM!
Shall we do the phone thing?
xoxo

E-mail is great if you want to send messages to your friends and aren't desperate for a quick reply - but wouldn't it be great if you could use a computer to talk to your mates in real time? Well, you can and it's called chat.

There are millions of chat-rooms all over the world wide web. Lots of sites have chat-rooms as part of their content, while some sites are dedicated to nothing but chat. It can be a long, hard slog to find a chat-room that you like. But it's worth it 'cause, if you're like any of the other millions of girls online, you'll probably end up using most of your webtime to chat. **We're girls, so we like to talk, so sue us!**

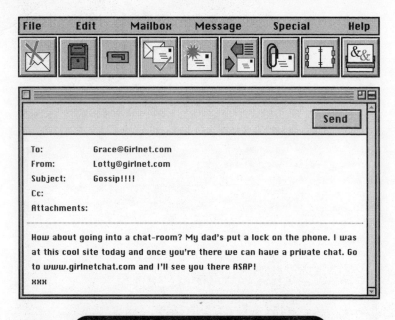

| File | Edit | Mailbox | Message | Special | Help |

Send

To: Grace@Girlnet.com
From: Lotty@girlnet.com
Subject: Gossip!!!!
Cc:
Attachments:

How about going into a chat-room? My dad's put a lock on the phone. I was at this cool site today and once you're there we can have a private chat. Go to www.girlnetchat.com and I'll see you there ASAP!
xxx

How to find cool chat sites

Just like in real life where you wouldn't want to spend hours of your time talking to boring adults about boring adult stuff, if you're looking for chat-rooms then it's best to go to sites that are for teenagers or kids. Some of the sites already mentioned, like Surf Monkey or Freezone, have safe, monitored chat, or you could do a search, using "teen chat" or "kids chat" as your keywords.

It's also worth thinking about what kind of people you want to meet in a chat-room. If you don't want to spend loads of time having to read messages from people slagging each other off and being rude, then go to a site that has safe surfing rules. You might have to become a member of the site before you're allowed into the chat-rooms but, rather than being a waste of time, this is a good way to make sure that the site is trying to make your chat experience a happy one. Like, the people using the chat-rooms won't misbehave if they know the webmaster has a record of their e-mail address.

If you're a big fan of a certain pop group or television programme or even an actor, check out their official site as they should have chat-rooms where you can type away for hours about your favourite obsession.

When you click on to a chat-room you should see an intro page before you get into the chat-room for real. You'll be asked for a nickname that you want to use in the chat-room. You'll probably be advised not to use your real name - **this is just another way of protecting you from any stupid types that love to stir it up**. You'll probably also be asked for your real name and your e-mail address, but whether or not you actually fill these boxes in should be up to you. It's best to leave them blank though as this information will be on show to anyone using the chat-room if they click on your name and ask for your details. Anyways after filling in your nickname you click on a button that says something like "connect" or "start chatting" and hopefully the chat window will load and you can chat away to your heart's content.

Sometimes chatting won't be so easy. If you're at school, chances are that your computer teach has built a "firewall" into the school 'puter system. Firewalls have now't to do with living flames, they're just a little technical device that blocks access to certain areas of the web. And teachers have funny ideas that you should use school computers for educational stuff but, hey, how boring is that?

If you're on a home computer and still have problems getting the chat to load, it could be because you need to download some chat software. Ah, downloads, pesky things, but not actually that difficult to do. If you're using an Apple computer then you're using different software to most people on the web. The site you're on will either tell you what you need to download and give you a link to click on and guide you through the downloading (it usually involves clicking on a few command boxes and waiting a couple of minutes for the software to arrive) or you might have to go to "edit" on your toolbar, move the cursor down to "preferences", click on something called Java (a computer language) and then click on a little box that says "enable Java". Which should take you approximately thirty seconds from start to finish.

If like most computer users you're using a PC that runs on a Windows programme (the most popular software in the world!), you shouldn't have too many problems.

But if you still can't get your chat thing going on, any decent chat site should have a help button you can click on and a list of FAQ (frequently asked questions) that you can have a look at to see what you're doing wrong.

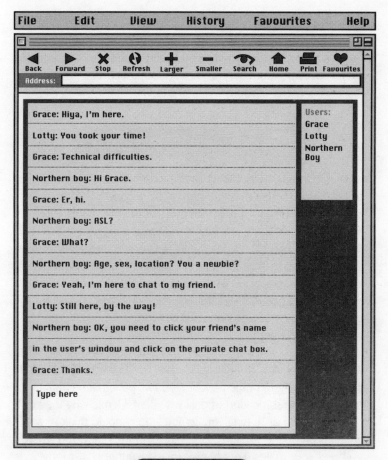

As Grace and Lotty just found out, there are a few things you need to know to make your chat stress-free. It'll take you a couple of minutes to suss out what's the what in your chat-room and don't get hissy if it takes a couple of visits before you get the hang of it. After all, it took a little patience to do the e-mail thing too and now you're a complete pro!

Most chat sites will have useful tips or a big help section that you can have a look at before you start chatting. They'll explain how to find out how many people are in a chat-room, how you can make a private chat-room for you and your mates and how to block chat messages from other users who are hacking you off.

This is what the chat-room will look like:

What's cool about chat?

You might wonder why chat is so great compared to e-mail or just talking to your mates over the phone. It's a good question. For a start, unlike e-mail, with chat you can talk to your mates in real time, that is as soon as you type a sentence and press a button your friend will be able to read what you wrote, instead of having to go into her e-mail set-up and see if she has any new messages. And unlike the telephone where your annoying sibs can listen in or your 'rents know full well that you're not talking about your history project, what you do in a chat-room is between you and the other chat users.

We've already talked about how e-mails let you write like you talk without worrying too much about stuff like punctuation and spelling. It's the same kind of deal with chat. Hence why they call it "chat" instead of "typing" or "writing". You should think of chat-rooms as an online version of the places in the real world where you meet your mates. Lots of girls have favourite chat-rooms where they arrange to meet their friends at certain times, just like going round to someone's house. Because most chat-rooms let you make your own personal chat-rooms, it means you and your

 buds can settle down for a good gossip, without having to worry about the other people using the chat-room to get the low down on your personal life or butt in where they're not wanted.

But although you can use chat-rooms as cyber hang-outs, it's also

File   Edit   View   History   Favourites   Help

◀ Back ▶ Forward ✕ Stop ↻ Refresh + Larger − Smaller 👁 Search 🏠 Home 🖨 Print ♥ Favourites

Address:

Users:
Grace
Lotty

Grace: Phew! Alone at last.

Lotty: At least that Northern boy showed us what to do.

Grace: Yeah he was sweet.

Lotty: But enough about him. What's going on with Claire and Matt?

Grace: Oh yeah! Well she went out with her mates yesterday to the cinema and caught him in the back row with another girl.

Lotty: Really?

Grace: Really!

Lotty: So what did she do?

Grace: Asked him what he was doing and he pretended that it was his cousin from out of town – but Claire accused him of lying.

Lotty: Then what happened?

Grace: She stormed out and she's been in a cranky bad mood ever since. And Matt keeps phoning her and she keeps telling me to tell him that he's dumped.

Lotty: But it could have been his cousin.

Grace: That's what I said and she told me to shut up.

Lotty: Claire can be such a witch sometimes. Do you reckon they'll get back together?

Grace: Yeah, 'course they will!

Type here

cool to go into chat-rooms and make new friends. It's called the world wide web 'cause it's truly world wide, so it's not uncommon to get chatting to someone from the USA or Australia or Sweden. And you don't even have to leave your house!

Netiquette

You already know that when you're e-mailing people, vowels and spelling words properly tend to go pear-shaped, but chat-room lingo is a completely different game. It's not so much that people write differently, but forget everything they were ever taught about capital letters and commas. It's that there's a whole strange language that people use in chat-rooms that takes a little getting used to.

The main difference is that people use initials to spell out phrases. Fr'instance BRB means "be right back", LOL means "laughing out loud" and "ASL?" means "age, sex, location" (how old are you, where do you live and are you a girl-shape or a boy-shape?). You'll be able to figure these out as you go along.

But what's the deal with those weird little symbols that people keep using that look like smiley faces :-) (if you look at 'em sideways)? They're called "emoticons" (which is a cross between emotions and icons) and they're a cute little way to let the other chatters know how you're feeling. Like, if you've just made a slightly sarky comment you might add an emoticon that looks like this: ;-) after the sentence to let people know you were winking and just being funny. There are hundreds and hundreds of emoticons and abbreviations that people use in chat and if you looks at Chapter Nine of this here book, we've listed a whole bunch of them so you can use them too!

When chat goes bad

If you take our chat advice then you'll have a good time in chat-rooms. Occasionally though, chat situations can get a little weird. It's a bit like real life. Sometimes you might be having a chat with someone, even a good friend, and they'll get all nasty for no apparent reason. But, unlike real life, where you end up going home and eating too much chocolate and getting all mopey, **there are things you can do if your chat experience goes a little bit grrrr.**

The first thing you should do is **always use a monitored chat-room,** if at all possible. These are chat-rooms where a member of staff is always keeping an eye on the chat to make sure people don't swear or get offensive. It doesn't mean that they're there to wig on your chats - it just means you've entered a safe environment.

Monitored chat-rooms will also make sure that all chatters are the same age and they may even send an e-mail to your parents to let them know that you've had the good sense and maturity to choose a safe chat site. (Actually, it's a pretty good idea to let the 'rents know where you're chatting 'cause they'll be more likely to let you use the net if they know where and what you're getting up to.) If you want to use a chat-room that's safe and kid-friendly try www.kidzone.com or other sites that practise safe surfing.

If you're on a site and another chatter keeps hassling you for private chat or being abusive, you should do two things. Firstly you should let the webmaster or the chat monitor know about this person and what stupid things they've been doing. And secondly you should highlight that person's name in your list of chatters and then click in the box that says "ignore" (or something similar). By doing this you make it impossible for them to communicate with you. It's really not worth worrying about this stuff. Most of the time you'll love chatting and if you remember our little checklist of chatting tips then you can't go wrong.

Ten rules for happy chatting:

1 **Never use your real name.**
It's always better to keep your identity hidden.

2 **Never give out your phone number.**
Most chat-rooms don't allow people to give out numbers, but you should also be aware that it's not sensible to give out your telephone number to someone who you've met in a chat-room.

3 **Never give out your address.**
The same goes for your address. Always remember to be safe and sussed.

4 **Don't arrange to meet someone you met in a chat-room.**
OK, you might think that this is the start of a beautiful friendship, but you should never, ever agree to meet someone from a chat-room unless you can get one of your parents to come with you.

5 **Don't believe everything people tell you in chat.**
Just as you told a boy you met in a chat-room that you were fifteen, blonde, blue-eyed and a part-time model, that boy might not be everything he said he was either.

6 **Don't flame people.**
If you're rude to people in chat-rooms you'll have all the other chatters yelling at you, plus you'll probably get kicked out of the room by the chat monitor. Oh and it's not very nice too.

7 **Use your "block chatter" option if you keep getting private messages.**
It can be really irritating to log on to a chat-room and before you've even had a chance to say "hi", you start getting

bombarded with "do you want to private chat" messages from creepy boys you don't even know. Put a block on them or make it clear that you're happy to talk to them but only in the main chat-room. And remember you can block out anyone who's causing you to get annoyed.

8 Do complain to the chat monitor if you think someone's out of order.

Don't worry about ratting on people. If they're out of order, then they should get booted. And don't worry about wasting the chat monitor's time - hey, it's what they're getting paid for!

9 Read the rules of the chat-room before you enter.

This will let you know what you can and can't do or talk about in the chat-room. Plus it will also give you some clues on whether the chat is well-run or not.

10 Try to use kids-only chat-rooms.

They're safe, monitored and dead, dead easy to use.

⑥ *Makeovers, screensavers, wallpaper and freebies*

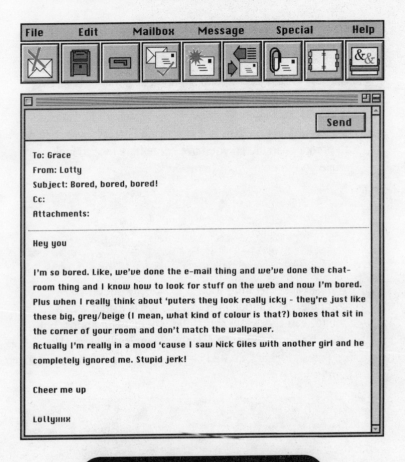

File   Edit   Mailbox   Message   Special   Help

Send

To: Grace
From: Lotty
Subject: Bored, bored, bored!
Cc:
Attachments:

Hey you

I'm so bored. Like, we've done the e-mail thing and we've done the chat-room thing and I know how to look for stuff on the web and now I'm bored. Plus when I really think about 'puters they look really icky - they're just like these big, grey/beige (I mean, what kind of colour is that?) boxes that sit in the corner of your room and don't match the wallpaper.
Actually I'm really in a mood 'cause I saw Nick Giles with another girl and he completely ignored me. Stupid jerk!

Cheer me up

Lottyxxx

Prettying up your 'puter

Lotty's right when she reckons that computers aren't exactly the most beautiful objects that a girl can have littering up her bedroom, unless you have a cutely coloured iMac that is. Computer designers are so busy thinking about what goes inside a 'puter that sometimes they forget the outside.

If you're lucky enough to have your very own computer - and don't have to share it with your entire family - there's no reason why you can't get creative and give your computer a makeover.

Eight makeover tips for your computer:

1 Stickers are an easy way to stamp your personality all over your 'puter. You could go to a sticker booth and make your own stickers featuring you and your mates, or find stickers with your favourite bands and cartoon characters to stick on the monitor frame so you have something nice to look at while you're doing your homework.

2 Don't use magnets. Yup, it would be nice to buy a magnetic poetry kit and compose rhymes while you're waiting for internet pages to download - but those little magnets will play havoc with your hard drive.

3 You can also buy furry frames to actually put on your computer so it suddenly looks like it has mated with a sheep. You should be able to find them in gift shops, but don't be surprised if the sales assistant looks at you like you've suddenly sprouted antlers when you ask if they stock 'em!

4 Glitter pens are great for drawing lil' pics of hearts and flowers all over your 'puter.

5 If your 'rents threaten to go ballistic if you even think of waving a felt tip anywhere near your computer, you can always arrange little objects on the top of it. A collection of novelty snowstorms, little cartoon figures or even that papier-mâché thingy you made in art class will look just dandy perched on top of your monitor.

6 Never ever cover up the air vents on the sides or back of your computer. Why? It will probably blow up if you do!

7 Find a cool song lyric or a line of poetry or even something really cool in an article in a magazine, use a nice typeface,

print it out on a piece of paper, cut it out and stick it on your
monitor frame. You'll feel inspired every time you look at it.

8 Alternatively you could do what most other people do and
decorate your computer and keyboard with a stunning
selection of apple cores, sweet wrappers and biscuit
crumbs!

That's the outside of your computer - but what about the inside?
Not the inside inside. There's no way you should be unscrewing
things and tinkering about with your circuit boards, but there's
loads of things you can customize to make your computer
completely different to everyone else's.

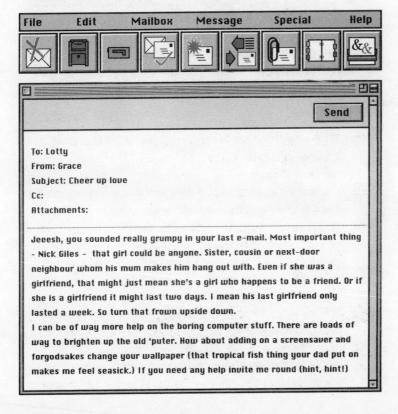

File   Edit   Mailbox   Message   Special   Help

Send

To: Lotty
From: Grace
Subject: Cheer up love
Cc:
Attachments:

Jeeesh, you sounded really grumpy in your last e-mail. Most important thing
- Nick Giles - that girl could be anyone. Sister, cousin or next-door
neighbour whom his mum makes him hang out with. Even if she was a
girlfriend, that might just mean she's a girl who happens to be a friend. Or if
she is a girlfriend it might last two days. I mean his last girlfriend only
lasted a week. So turn that frown upside down.
I can be of way more help on the boring computer stuff. There are loads of
way to brighten up the old 'puter. How about adding on a screensaver and
forgodsakes change your wallpaper (that tropical fish thing your dad put on
makes me feel seasick.) If you need any help invite me round (hint, hint!)

Wallpaper

No it's not what the walls of your room are papered with. This is desktop wallpaper, which is the background image on your computer. You might find that there are different wallpaper designs built into your 'puter software but they're probably fairly sucky - so get on to the net and find something that suits you. A couple of good websites to check out are www.free-wallpaper.to/ or www.free-wallpaper-art.com that will have thousands of images for you to download. They've got everything from movie wallpapers to popstars and even really weird psychedelic art designs. But you don't have to get your desktop wallpaper from a specific website. As you're surfing the net you can use any image that takes your fancy as wallpaper. You can even scan in a picture from a magazine or from your holiday snaps and use that as wallpaper. Once you've either downloaded the wallpaper or the image you want to use just follow our simple instructions and your desktop need never look boring again.

PC users:

To use a whole webpage as your wallpaper
1. Click the right-hand side button on your mouse and choose the "Use Wallpaper" option.

To use a smaller image
1. Download the image by clicking down with your mouse button and using the "Download Image to Disk" option.
2. Find the image and put it into the paint program.
3. Then click on edit and scroll down to the "Set as Wallpaper" option.

MAC USERS:

1. Download the image straight on to your desktop.
2. Click on the apple in the left-hand corner of your screen and scroll down to Control Panels.
3. Choose "Appearance", then choose "Desktop".
4. Click on "Place Picture", find the picture that you've downloaded and click on "Set Desktop".

Both PCs and Macs will let you play around with the picture
that you've chosen as your desktop pattern. You can stretch it so
it fills the whole screen or even tile it so you have a pretty pattern.
You might need to have a couple of practise runs, but once you
get the hang of it
you'll be changing
your wallpaper every
half an hour.

Screensavers

Screensavers are the little movies that pop up when your
machine's idling 'cause you've gone to the loo or to make a cup of
tea. They're a little trickier to install but nothing you can't handle.

There are loads of free screensavers on the net. One of the best
sites is www.screensaverlinks.com which will guide you to the best
screensaver sites. Also worth checking out is the official Daria site
www.daria.mtv.com which has some fantastic downloadable
goodies or www.spdownloads.com for South Park stuff, but if you
like your celebrities 'toon-like then www.celebrity screensavers.co.uk
is the first place you should look. And the best thing is that all these
screensavers should be yours for free. Ain't life grand? Once
you've decided on the screensaver you want, you need to
download and install it. Most sites will probably have a little guide
on how to do this or you could follow the instructions below.

PC users:

1. Download the file, making note of the directory you
   download to.
2. When the download is complete, use Windows Explorer to
   run the file by double-clicking on it.

The program will automatically copy the screensaver to the
correct location and make it your active screensaver.

MAC USERS:

1. Download the file to your desktop.
2. When the downloading is done, find the file.
3. Double-click on the file and open it on your desktop.
4. Drag the file to the Control Panels folder in your System Folder.
5. Reboot your Mac.
6. You can change your screensaver settings from the Control Panels menu.

Once you get the hang of screensavers there are a ton of other ways to personalize your computer. You could have a go at downloading and installing soundplugs, so instead of getting a beep when you make a mistake or have new e-mail you could have a little voice coming out of your computer. Or you could even download a spiffy web browser design, instead of the normal Netscape or Explorer browser windows. You can even download a whole new set of icons to use instead of the normal hard disk, e-mail and internet icons that most computers have.

It's a case of going online to have a good nose around at what's out there and not being afraid to have a bash at installing new things. If you get really stuck you can always consult your 'puter manual, e-mail the site that you're downloading things from to ask their advice or ask your computer teacher. But the best way to find out how to do things is experiment.

One word of warning: Keep a track of the actual size of the applications you're installing. Screensavers especially take up a load of space on your hard disk and you don't want to have so many cool, personalised details on your computer that you can't actually use it anymore! It kinda defeats the whole purpose of the exercise.

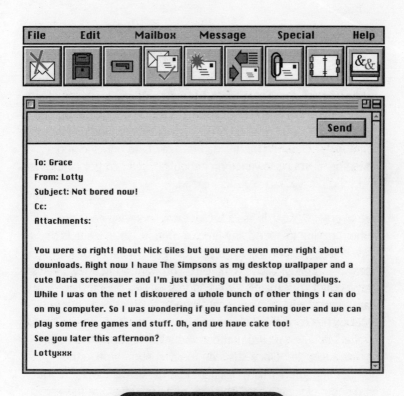

| File | Edit | Mailbox | Message | Special | Help |

Send

To: Grace
From: Lotty
Subject: Not bored now!
Cc:
Attachments:

You were so right! About Nick Giles but you were even more right about downloads. Right now I have The Simpsons as my desktop wallpaper and a cute Daria screensaver and I'm just working out how to do soundplugs. While I was on the net I diskovered a whole bunch of other things I can do on my computer. So I was wondering if you fancied coming over and we can play some free games and stuff. Oh, and we have cake too!
See you later this afternoon?
Lottyxxx

Free net goodies

After surfing around for dinky downloadables you'll realise that the net is a bit like a trolley dash in a really cool supermarket. There are so many things that you can take away and put on your own computer and you won't have to pay a pretty penny for any of it. The internet is a community, a sharing, looking-out-for-people type of community - so if someone invents an amazing piece of software they like to put it on the net and give it away to anyone who wants it for free. Hence the name, freeware.

But it's not just desktop downloadables that you can get your mitts on. Oh no. You think of it and it's probably already on the net, waiting to be double-clicked on by you.

Virtual cards and gifts

Oh dear, it's your mate's birthday and you completely forgot to get her a card. Or you've had a big fight and you know it's your fault, but you're too much of a scaredy cat to phone her up and apologize. Or you know she's upset about something and needs some major cheering up. Instead of rushing to her side and spending all your allowance on chocolate, you can get on the net and send her virtual presents instead.

Virtual greetings cards are a brilliant way of saying you care without having to spend any time or money. Go to a site like www.ecards.com or www.virtualgreetings.com for cards for every occasion. You just click on the card you want, fill in a few details like you and your mate's e-mail addresses and the message you want to send and then your card's good to go. When your mate receives her card she'll either be able to open it up on her e-mail or she'll be given a card number and a link to the virtual card service's website. Once she's on the site, she'll type in the number and get her card. It's a lot less hassle than going to the card shop, picking a card, thinking of a witty message to write in the card, stamping it and posting it.

If you're planning a party you can even send out your invites via the net if you go to www.alloy.com . But the best cards on the net have to be the animated Hello Kitty cards at www.sanrio.com . If you got one of these babies in your mailbox, it'd be guaranteed to put a smile on your face for the rest of the day.

Cards aren't the only virtual goodies to be found in cyberspace. You can also send your mates virtual gifts. You can choose from bouquets of flowers to cookies and chocolate and even cuddly toys. If you can think of a gift, chances are that somewhere on the internet is a virtual version of it just waiting to be sent to one of your buds. Some sites that you may want to check out include www.virtualbouquet.com, www.meetgreeks.com and www.greetsomeone.com/gifts/gifts.htm .

Free pets!

One of the most popular net crazes are virtual pets. If you have your own webpage (we'll talk about that in the next chapter) you can download your virtual pet on to it. But lots of sites have cyber pets that you can download straight on to your desktop so you can keep an eye on their welfare while you're writing e-mails or doing your science homework.

One of the most popular sites is www.neopets.com .Neopets don't look like your ordinary cats or dogs - instead they're weird, mutant-looking creatures who can get up to all sorts of mischief if they're not looked after properly. If you are after something a little more traditional and dog-shaped try www.puffin.ptialaska.net/youngs/dogs.htm or if cyber babies are more your bag then www.members.tripod.com/~Sherilynn/netbabies.html is where to get your non-puking, non-weeing little baby.

There are even more sites that will let you adopt everything from nerds to ghosts to dragons and even a goth girl called Tina The Troubled Teen (although she might be a little too close to home!). The best thing to do is to go to a search engine and do a keyword search for something like "virtual pets", "cyber pets" or "virtual adoption". And if you're the kind of girl who's not big on responsibility (and let's face it, who is?) then you might want to start off with something simple like a fish. So go to www.petfish.com and download a desktop guppy for free. Oh and try not to overfeed it!

Free games!

While we're on the hunt for free stuff, it's worth scouting for free games that you can either play online or download on to your computer - so you can wile away the hours without totting up a mammoth phone bill. Instead of hunting out free games on sites that you already visit, the best trick is to go to a site that specialises in games. Then you can scroll down huge lists of games and pick whatever takes your fancy.

Some sites even let you play online with other players. These are called multi-player games and it's a bit like going into a chat-room, but instead of chatting you can play scrabble or a shoot-'em-up game that involves killing off all your opponent's characters. There are so many free games sites that it would take the rest of this book just to list half of them, so try out the sites we have listed and they should have links to take you to yet more games sites. Meanwhile bookmark www.freefungames.com , www.freegames.com , www.free-games-net.com and www.Freegamesweb.com .

Even more free stuff

In this chapter we've talked about all the free stuff just waiting for you to double-click on it, but there are some sites that have everything on them: screensavers, wallpapers, games, pets, e-cards and everything from coupons you can print out to get money off things in the real world (that funny place that exists away from your 'puter). You might not be able to find exactly what you're looking for but they're a good place to start. www.netutopia.com/freebies/index.html , www.coolfreebies.com and www.gentlewhisper.com will open your eyes to a whole world of net freebies that will have you wrinkling your brow in amazement that people actually give this stuff away. But don't lose any sleep over it, just enjoy it while you can.

Oh, before you go on the net to grab your free goodies, remember to take loads of screen breaks otherwise you'll be seeing dots in front of your eyes - and open a window occasionally and get a couple of lungfuls of fresh air. Which, although you can't download it on to your 'puter, is free too!

⑦ How to make your own website

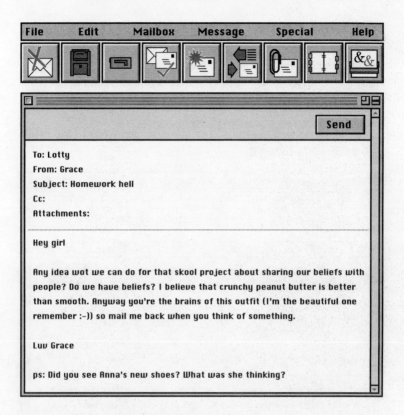

To: Lotty
From: Grace
Subject: Homework hell
Cc:
Attachments:

Hey girl

Any idea wot we can do for that skool project about sharing our beliefs with people? Do we have beliefs? I believe that crunchy peanut butter is better than smooth. Anyway you're the brains of this outfit (I'm the beautiful one remember :-)) so mail me back when you think of something.

Luv Grace

ps: Did you see Anna's new shoes? What was she thinking?

Not all websites are professionally created sites for products and telly shows. If you've been surfing the net for longer than five minutes you're bound to have come across ordinary people's websites. They might not be able to spend vast sums of money and use fancy shmancy little tricks to make their pages animated or play "The Charge of the Light Brigade" everytime you click on something, but usually personal homepages are so interesting 'cause you're getting to have a little peek into someone else's life. It's a bit like reading someone else's diary without having to worry that

a) they've been writing nasty things about you
b) and they're going to have a hissy fit if they find out.
Websites are there solely for other people to have a nose around them.

And because no one actually owns the internet, anyone in the world can put stuff on it. And they do. Think of a subject from Scottie dogs to tiddlywinks and there's bound to be a website devoted to it. You don't need any special qualifications or secret skills to make a website - which is why there's so darn many of 'em! So maybe it's time for you to think about making a little bit of the world wide web yours by creating your own website. **Admit it, it's a tempting thought!**

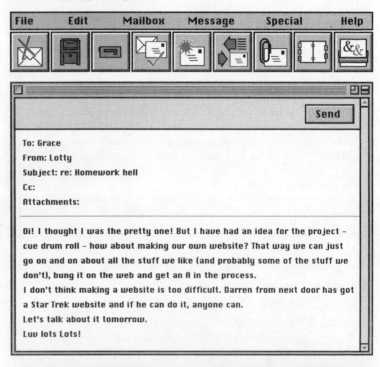

| File | Edit | Mailbox | Message | Special | Help |

Send

To: Grace
From: Lotty
Subject: re: Homework hell
Cc:
Attachments:

Oi! I thought I was the pretty one! But I have had an idea for the project – cue drum roll – how about making our own website? That way we can just go on and on about all the stuff we like (and probably some of the stuff we don't), bung it on the web and get an A in the process.
I don't think making a website is too difficult. Darren from next door has got a Star Trek website and if he can do it, anyone can.
Let's talk about it tomorrow.
Luv lots Lots!

What's your website going to be about?

Before you start worrying about how to actually make a website (which will actually be a worry-free exercise anyway, promise), you need to decide what your website is going to be about.
It could simply be about you and your life - almost like an online journal - as long as you don't mind people reading it. Lots of

websites are simply about people's passions or obsessions, however weird or strange they are. And, boy, do they get strange.

Ten weirdest website topics:

1 **Angels**
There are a ton of sites dedicated to angels - as some people believe that the winged messengers exist. So they post stories and anecdotes of angels saving small children in peril - and even have pictures of what they think angels look like.

2 **Corgi dogs**
Not just corgis but Labradors and Dachshunds too - 'cause some webmasters love their furry friends so much that they dress them up in funny costumes and put their pictures on the www.

3 **Anything to do with aliens**
Because the truth is out there...

4 **Cheese**
Not just something to put on your toast, but even the subject of websites. Check out www.ilovecheese.com if you share the obsession.

5 **Hanson fan fiction**
They might be a cool group who know a good tune, but lots of Hanson fans even write stories about the singing brothers, where they save the world, snog a lot and still find time to be in a pop group.

6 Sugarcrafting
Icing sugar is good on cakes but some odd types like to make sculptures out of it and display their work on the internet. Why, why, why?

7 Dancing babies, dancing hamsters, dancing cats
Every now and then a craze spreads among the web community. A few years ago it was a small download of a computer-generated, nappy-wearing baby dancing to music, then it was cartoon hamsters. Who knows where it will end?

8 Slushy romance novels
Readers of those books your gran probably reads (which always have women in crinolines snogging dashing men on the cover) have taken over a small corner of the web. And in that scary corner they review their favourite books (which all seem to have the same plot anyway) and play swapsies. Grow up, grandma!

9 Unicorns
A bit like the Angel sites, but these dudes believe that unicorns really exist and insist on scanning in pastel watercolours featuring horned horses and the like.

10 Second-hand clothes
You know that you can buy new clothes on the web, but did you know you could also buy second-hand (or vintage) threads on the net too? Well, you do now!

So you see, it doesn't matter how bizarre your website might be, there'll be a home for it online. And it doesn't even have to be that strange. You could have a celebrity fan-site, so you can let everyone know just how much you love **Freddie Prinze Jr**, or a music site where you can post your own Top Tens and music reviews. Or you can just tell the world about you, your mates, your pets and why you really can't stand pigeons. The choice is yours.

Plan, baby, plan

It's still not time to actually build your website. You have to do some planning first. Once you've decided what you want your site to be about you have to think about some practical stuff which will make your life way easier once you start creating webpages for real.

1 How big will your site be?

Do you want your site to consist of just one page or do you want that first page to link to four other sections which will all be five pages long? It helps to draw something called a site-map so you can be clear in your head what your site will look like and how people will be able to find their way (or navigate your pages).

2 What is your site going to look like?

What colours do you want your site to have and do they go together? What kind of lettering do you want? And will the colours and the typeface you've chosen give people a headache when they come to your site? These are all decisions you'll have to make, oh webmistress.

3 Are you going to have pictures on your site?

If you want pictures on your site (and it would look pretty spiffy if you did), you'll need to take some photos or maybe do some illustrations and scan them in. You might even be able to take pictures off other sites, but you'll have to check with the site owner first.

4 How much content will your site have?

Time to think about the words now. If you have lots and lots

of text is anyone going to be bothered to squint their eyes
and read it? Unlike books and magazines, staring at a 'puter
screen for long amounts of time can give you a headache
and funny spots in front of your eyes, so it could be a good
idea to do the whole "less is more" thing and keep your
words to a minimum. They can still be funny an' all - there
just won't be quite so many of them.

5 Be inspired

If you're having trouble building a picture of what you want
your site to be or how you want it to look, get on the net
and have a surf around to suss out sites you like. Try to think
about why you like them. Maybe there's a cool design idea
that you could use on your site or you particularly dig the
way someone's written their online diary.

The no-tears way to makin' a website

By now you should have a firm idea of what your site will be about
and how it's going to look. All you have to do is build the darn
thing. Gulp. But this website malarkey is not as difficult as it looks.
Think about it, if it was that hard to do, this whole internet thing
would never have caught on in the first place. Like so much else
there are easy and hard ways to make a website. Let's start with
the easier methods and work our way up.

1 Get someone else to do it for you.

Sounds too good to be true but there are actually people out
there who'll make your site for you. If you want a very
simple site that just says who you are and what you're into
then it's possible to get a nethead to do everything else. If
you're under fifteen simply go to
www.angelfire.com/de/fkhp/ and give them some info about
your good self, then they'll do the rest. They'll even set up a
free e-mail account for you.

Use a free website-building service.

Lots of big websites like Yahoo and Lycos actually provide a free service where you can build your own website and they'll host it (put it on the web for you). When you register at their site you'll have access to web-building tools (which don't involve any coding), be able to use their graphics and artwork and get fancy software for your site so you can have surveys, polls and even chat-rooms if you want. Interested? Check out www.xoom.com, www.geocities.com (owned by Yahoo) or www.angelfire.com (owned by Lycos).

 Use web-building software.

When you buy a new computer you usually get free software packages thrown in. Now one of these clever little software packages will be a web-page building programme. If you have a PC, your web software will probably be called Frontline Express and if you have a Mac, your software will be Adobe Pagemill. It's very easy to use, again you don't have to try and get your head around any coding and you'll be able to access FAQ and instruction manuals to help you along the way. Once you've built your site you can either go to one of the internet-based web-hosting sites mentioned above or contact your ISP and they'll be able to get your little creation live on the www.

 Build the thing from scratch.

If you're up for it and feeling brave you can always build your site by learning to code. Websites use a programming language called HTML which stands for Hypertext Markup Language. HTML tells the web browser how to display the text on websites. Fr'instance it will tell the web browser that certain words should be in bold or should be blue or bigger than other words. Really simply how it works is by putting words into tags, using the tag keys on your keyboard which look like this: < >.

There are lots of sites on the web that will teach you how to HTML (and most people who use it swear you can learn the basics in an hour) but one of the best sites is www.gurlpages.com which has helped thousands of girls put up their own sites on gurlpages. Their guide is the perfect, hand-holding way to learn about HTML for a beginner. And if you visit the computer section of your local bookshop have a look for a book called **HTML for Dummies**, which is the easiest and friendliest HTML manual you'll ever read (if you were actually planning on reading more than one, that is).

NB: If you're interested in how HTML works, next time you're on the web, click on "View" in your toolbar and then click on "Source" and you'll be able to see the HTML language that the webpage was written in. One of the coolest things about using "Source" is if you see a nice little layout on someone else's website, but you can't work out how they did it, by using "Source" you can find out what the HTML code was and use it yourself. (I'm sure they won't mind.)

Advanced coders only!

If you're a whizz at HTML and want to give your site really cutting-edge graphics, then there are more web-coding languages you can learn like Javascript and Flash. These more advanced programmes will animate your site so you can have moving graphics and sound. And as well as the free software packages that came with your 'puter, you can also buy software like Dreamweaver which experienced web designers (that'd be people who actually do this for a living) use. But be warned, they ain't cheap!

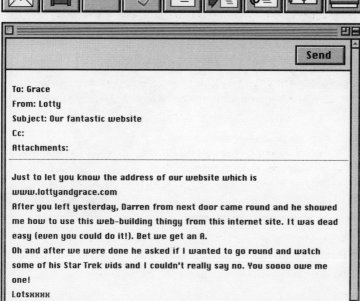

To: Grace
From: Lotty
Subject: Our fantastic website
Cc:
Attachments:

Just to let you know the address of our website which is
www.lottyandgrace.com
After you left yesterday, Darren from next door came round and he showed
me how to use this web-building thingy from this internet site. It was dead
easy (even you could do it!). Bet we get an A.
Oh and after we were done he asked if I wanted to go round and watch
some of his Star Trek vids and I couldn't really say no. You soooo owe me
one!
Lotsxxxx

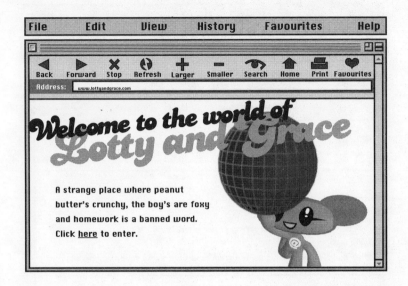

| File | Edit | View | History | Favourites | Help |

Back   Forward   Stop   Refresh   Larger   Smaller   Search   Home   Print   Favourites

Address: www.lottyandgrace.com

Welcome to the world of Lotty and Grace

A strange place where peanut
butter's crunchy, the boy's are foxy
and homework is a banned word.
Click <u>here</u> to enter.

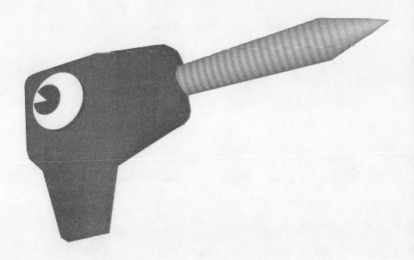

⑧ The internet and beyond

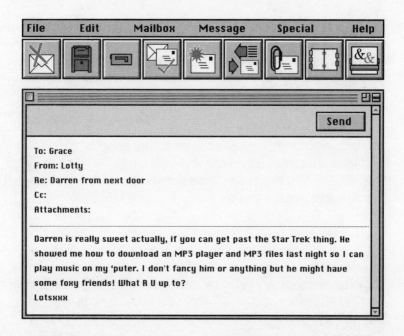

There are a few more goodies to be had from the internet that you really should know about. As well as cool websites there's also software (little computer programmes) that you can download for free that are so clever you'll wonder how you managed to live without them.

MP3s and WINAMPS

Although most computers now come with a built in CD player so you can play music while you surf, there are also computer applications you can download which act like CD players and store way more music. The most well known is "MP3" which stands for Motion Picture Experts Group audio layer 3. MP3 files can store music in one twelfth of the space of CDs, for faster downloading and easy storage. If you go to a site called www.MP3.com you can download MP3 player software to install on your 'puter (which is dead easy to do) and then download lots of songs to actually play on it.

There are lots of sites that have MP3 song files for you to download, but you have to be careful as unless the sites have the permission of the bands and their record companies it can be illegal for you to download the files. But, luckily, a lot of groups are tech-heads themselves and want to give something back to the fans, so they make sure that some of their songs or special previews of unreleased tracks are available for download on the internet. The best way to find these musical gems is to go to the band's official website and see if they have any MP3 files.

If you really get into the MP3 thing, you can even buy a portable MP3 player (they cost about the same as a portable CD player) so you can store and play your MP3 files while you're taking a walk down to the shops. MP3 players are about the size of a walkman and use Flash Memory Cards to store the sound files on.

"Winamps" are pretty much the same as MP3 players but they only work on computers which use Windows software. Again, they're a piece of software that you install on your computer and use like a CD player. And unlike MP3s, you can play CDs on a Winamp (although you can play MP3 files too).

To get a free Winamp download go to www.winamp.com. Although winamps look pretty boring - as you can see below:

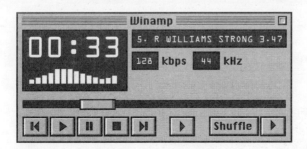

You can also download winamp skins from the internet to make your little winamp window look far more pretty and interesting. There are literally thousands of skins to choose from, but a good place to start would be a search engine where you need to type in "free winamp skins" as your keyword search.

Of course you could always use the CD player that's built into your 'puter - but what's the point of having all this swank technology if you never use it?

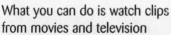

Moving pictures

You can also watch moving images on your computer too. Theoretically you could watch an entire movie, but it would take hours to download and you'd definitely get sore eyes (although in a couple of years computers and tellies will be the same thing so it may be possible).

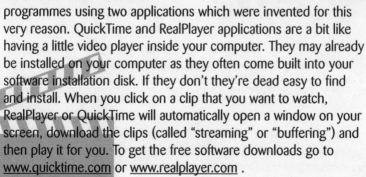

What you can do is watch clips from movies and television programmes using two applications which were invented for this very reason. QuickTime and RealPlayer applications are a bit like having a little video player inside your computer. They may already be installed on your computer as they often come built into your software installation disk. If they don't they're dead easy to find and install. When you click on a clip that you want to watch, RealPlayer or QuickTime will automatically open a window on your screen, download the clips (called "streaming" or "buffering") and then play it for you. To get the free software downloads go to www.quicktime.com or www.realplayer.com .

And to find sites that have RealPlayer or QuickTime clips, go to any official TV or movie website (yup, keyword search time again!). But remember to have something interesting to read while you're waiting for the clips to download!

Even more ways to chat

E-mail and chat are amazing inventions but the web can also provide you with even more smart ways to gab with your mates. One of the best-kept web secrets and one of the most useful is instant chat. Like chat-rooms you can talk to your mates in real time without sending e-mails and having to wait for a reply, but with instant chat you don't even have to go to a chat-room, you just have to be online.

When you subscribe to an instant chat service like Hotmail's Instant Messenger Service (you should see a little link for it on the Hotmail homepage at www.hotmail.com), you download and install a little piece of software and you're good to go. You give the Instant Messenger Service the Hotmail addresses of your mates (they have to be on Hotmail for it to work) and then Instant Messenger will e-mail them and tell them how to install it.

Then every time you go online, you open your little Instant Messenger box, see if any of your friends are connected to the internet and if they are you can chat to them. As long as you're online, the Instant Messenger box lets you and your mates chat, without having to arrange a chat-room to meet in.

ICQ is fairly similar to Instant Messenger but you don't need a Hotmail account to use it. It's probably the most well-known Instant Chat device on the web - millions and millions of net users subscribe to ICQ. If you go to the website at www.icq.com and download and install the ICQ software on to your computer (it's a little bit trickier than Instant Messenger but they give you loads of help and instructions), you'll be given an ICQ number. You can then do an ICQ search on your mates by looking for their names or e-mail addresses on the ICQ search engine. Or you could e-mail them and tell them to join ICQ sharpish. Once you've got a gang of mates all ICQ-ed up, you add their ICQ numbers to your list and when you go online and open your ICQ box, like Instant Messenger, it will tell you if any of your buds are around.

With ICQ, as well as chatting, you can also send your mates e-mails or even post them website addresses. And again you don't need to go into a chat-room to keep in touch with your friends. ICQ's website has loads of other cool things on it, if you happen to be passing, including chat-rooms, friendship pages and online stories that you can write with different people from around the world.

Phone fun

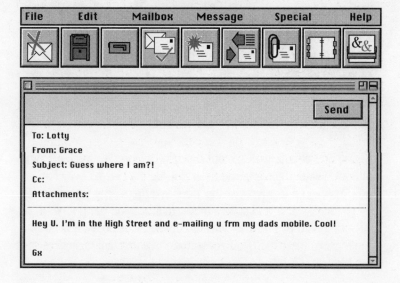

File   Edit   Mailbox   Message   Special   Help

Send

To: Lotty
From: Grace
Subject: Guess where I am?!
Cc:
Attachments:

Hey U. I'm in the High Street and e-mailing u frm my dads mobile. Cool!

Gx

You don't have to be sitting in front of a computer to use the internet either. Now you can go online via your mobile phone. Unfortunately most mobiles aren't connected to the web. But if you have a WAP phone you can phone and surf.

"WAP" (which stands for Wireless Application Protocol if you're interested) is a digital communications system that lets you access the internet and send and read e-mails from your mobile. Obviously your mobile is a tiny, wee thing compared to the average 'puter and you'd probably end up with a squint and/or very bad eyesight if you tried to look at most webpages on your phone screen. So the internet services that are provided for WAP phones are specially selected. Fr'instance you wouldn't necessarily want to read some fan fiction on your mobile phone (all those words would give you a raging headache) but you might want to find out what the weather's going to be like later that day, or get the footie scores or even read your horoscope.

Something you don't need a WAP phone for is "text messaging", which is like e-mailing but using your phone keypad instead. If you're lucky enough to have a mobile phone then you're probably already addicted to texting - but did you know you can send people text messages via the internet? Yup, it's true!

Imagine one of your mates is out shopping and you're stuck at home but decide you're going to meet her outside the cinema in half an hour. You can go to a website that does text messaging (preferably free text messaging) and send a message straight to her phone. If that sounds like your bag try www.breathe.com or do a keyword search using, that's right you guessed it, "free text messaging" as your keyword search.

Lots of companies are wising up to how much we're attached to our phones and in the future expect to get lots of text messages from companies advertising their products. Soon we'll be able to get text messages from our favourite websites and companies with special offers and pieces of gossip coming direct to our mobiles.

Web TV

It's not just your mobile phone that can connect you to the internet - your telly can too! Interactive television is the latest thing after satellite and digital TV. It works by using a satellite which is hovering somewhere in space, a box which sits on top of your television and your telephone line to send communication between your TV and the interactive service.

Not only do you get to watch TV (which is always cool), interactive television lets you send e-mails to your mates and buy the CD of the band you've just seen being interviewed. You don't use your remote control though - it would be a bit hard to write an e-mail using the volume button - but a keyboard that you get when you subscribe to the service. But to get interactive television would involve you making puppy dog eyes at the 'rental units and trying to persuade them that it would be really educational if they subscribed to an interactive television service.

Well, interactive television isn't strictly educational, but the things that you can do with it might help you with your homework. Fr'instance if you were watching a programme about dinoasaurs and they flagged up a website address, instead of scrabbling for a piece of paper you could go straight on to the internet while you watched the programme. You can also get access to information about dinosaurs from the programme makers in the form of additional text boxes that come up onscreen and even e-mail a question to the presenter. If you were watching a football match you could choose different camera angles, call up information on all the players and even order your own instant action replay.

To the future and beyond...

In a couple of years time, the internet will be even bigger, better and, erm, brighter than it is now. It will take less time to download pages and new technology that is being developed right now will allow you to do everything from e-mail your homework straight into your school's database to being able to go on dates with an interactive boyfriend who you control.

Instead of having separate television and computers, we'll have terminals (probably in every room, apart from maybe the toilet) which will allow us to go online and watch telly, check our e-mails, chat to our mates, put on the central heating and make doctor's appointments for us.

Who knows what else the internet will be able to do, but one thing's for sure - it's going to be fun finding out!

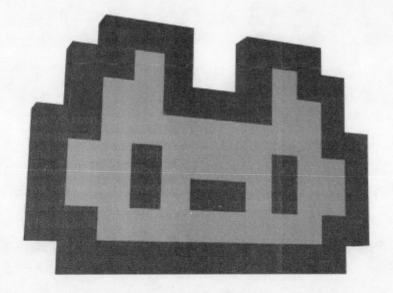

⑨ Emoticons, web-words and other techie-speak explained

This chapter should be used as a handy glossary or dictionary for any of those baffling words or symbols you might find on the web which cause you to scrunch your face up and go, "Huh?"

Emoticons

In Chapter Five (which was all about chat-rooms if you can't remember that far back) emoticons were mentioned. They're the little symbols you can make using the punctuation keys on your keyboard to show others how you're feeling. There are hundreds and hundreds of emoticons and here is a darn big list of them for you to use and recognise. (It helps to look at them with your head tilted sideways.)

Feelgood emoticons

:-) A basic smiley face used to show people that you're only joking.

;-) Winking smiley used to show a flirty or sarky remark.

:'-) I'm so happy that I'm crying.

3:] Pet smiley.

:-D I'm laughing.

||*(I'm offering to shake hands.

||*) I'm accepting a handshake.

Not so feel good emoticons

:-(Frowning smiley to show that someone is feeling mopey.

:-I Indifferent smiley. Slightly better than a frowning smiley but not much.

:-> I've just made a really biting sarcastic remark.

>:-> I've just made a really devilish remark.

;-> Winky and devilish combined.

:'-(I'm crying.

:-@ I'm screaming.

:-r I'm blowing a raspberry.

:-f I'm sticking my tongue out.

Downright weird emoticons

>. I'm a girl.

:- I'm a boy.

(-: I'm left-handed.

%-) I've been been staring at a 'puter screen for fifteen hours straight.

[:] I'm a robot.

8-)   I'm wearing sunglasses.

B:-) I'm wearing sunglasses on my head.

::-) I'm wearing glasses.

B-)   I'm wearing horn-rimmed glasses.

8:-) I'm a little girl.

:-{) I've got a moustache.

:-{} I'm wearing lipstick.

{:-) I'm wearing a wig.

}:-(I'm wearing a wig and standing in an updraft.

:-[I'm a vampire.

:-E   I'm a bucktoothed vampire.

:-F   I'm a bucktoothed vampire with one tooth missing.

:-*   I just ate something sour.

:-)~ I'm dribbling.

:-~) I've got a cold.

:-#   I'm wearing braces.

:^)   I've got a broken nose.

:v)	I've got a broken nose, but it's the other way.
:-&	I'm tongue-tied.
- - -:-)	I'm a punk rocker.
- - -:-(	Real punk rockers don't smile.
:=)	I've got two noses.
+-:-)	I'm the Pope.
`:-)	I shaved one of my eyebrows off this morning.
,:-)	Same thing ... other side.
|-I	I'm asleep.
|-O	I'm yawning/snoring.
O-)	I'm a scuba diver.
O :-)	I'm an angel (at heart, at least).
:-P	Nyahhhh!
:-S	I've just made an incoherent statement.
:-X	My lips are sealed.
:-C	I'm really bummed.
3:[	Mean Pet smiley.
:-9	I'm licking my lips.
%-6	I'm brain-dead.

[:-)	I'm wearing a walkman.
(:I	I'm an egghead.
<:-I	I'm a dunce.
:-0	No Yelling!
:-:	Mutant Smiley.
|.-)	I only have one eye.
8 :-)	I'm a wizard.
&:-)	I have curly hair.
C=}>;*{))	Mega-Smiley ... A drunk, devilish chef with a toupee in an updraft, a moustache and a double chin.
K:P	I'm a little kid with a propeller beanie.

Mini emoticons (for when time is short)

:)	Happy.
:(	Sad.
:>	What?
:@	Whaaaaaat!?
:I	Hmmm...
:[	Real Downer.

:O	Yelling.
:,(	Crying.
[]	Hugs and ...
:*	Kisses.
|I	Asleep.
^o	Snoring.
|-)	Ha ha.
|-)	Hee hee.
|-D	Ho ho.
:->	Hey hey.
:O	Oops.

Abbreviations

Life is short and expensive on the web - especially when your parents are yelling about the phone bill. Use these abbreviations on e-mail or chat and save time and money!

ASL - Age, sex, location.
BBL - Be back later.
BRB - Be right back.
CU - See you!
ROTFL - Rolling on the floor laughing.
RTM - Read the manual!
XOXO - Hugs and kisses.

Tech-speak deciphered

Bothered by all that cyber-speak? Be bothered no more with the **Girl Net** handy guide to techie terms.

@

A short way to say "at" in an e-mail address.

Attachment

A file which is sent with an e-mail. It could be anything from a word file to a scanned-in picture. You can tell if any e-mails you receive have attachments because you'll see a little paper clip symbol.

Browser

A browser is a 'puter programme that converts coded webpaged pages into regular words and pictures so that you can see them.

CD Rom

A CD Rom (or Compact Disk Read-Only Memory) looks like a music CD but carries computer data instead of sound.

Chat

Sending text messages to someone else in real time.

Cookie

A piece of information sent by a web-server to your browser. (A web-server is the computer that "hosts" a website and responds to requests from a user's browser.) Cookies may include information such as login or registration identification and your likes and dislikes. The browser saves the information and sends it back to the web-server whenever the browser returns to the website. The web-server may use the cookie to personalize the display it sends to you, or it may keep track of the different pages within the site that you use.

Cursor

The little arrow on the screen which you can move around.

Cyber space

A cool expression for the world wide web.

Data

A techie word for information. It can be either numbers or words.

Dial-up

A connection to the internet via a telephone line.

Download

To copy information or files from the internet on to your own computer.

E-commerce

E, or electronic, commerce means buying, selling and advertizing on the world wide web.

E-mail

Short for electronic mail and is a message sent between two computers over the internet.

FAQ (Frequently Asked Questions)

Pages which list and answer the questions most often asked about a website, computer programme or newsgroup.

File

Anything you save on the computer such as a software program, document or picture becomes a file. It's the 'puter version of the paper stuff that people put in filing cabinets.

Firewall

Software that prevents people from looking at certain websites by blocking their access.

Flaming

Posting or sending a deliberately rude or offensive message via newsgroup, e-mail.

Freeware

Freeware is software that's available on the internet by its maker for no charge.

FTP - (File Transfer Protocol)

A way of transferring files over the internet from one computer to another.

Hard disk

The part of a computer which stores all your data.

Hardware

What your computer is - which includes the techie inside stuff, the monitor, keyboard and mouse, as well as other equipment like printers and speakers.

Homepage

The first page on a website, which introduces the site and provides the means of navigation.

HTML

HTML (Hypertext Mark-up Language)
All the pages on the internet are written in HTML, which is a very complicated programming language of codes, symbols and tags that is shared between computers. Fortunately your web browser translates HTML into words and pictures so you don't have to!

HTTP (Hypertext Transfer Protocol)

This is the protocol (or set of codes) which allows the HTML document to be sent over the internet. That is why all webpage addresses start http:// (if you were wondering).

Internet

The internet is a network which connects computers to each other so they can share files and data.

ISP

Internet Service Provider - a company that gives you access to the internet either for free or for money.

LINK (or Hypertext Link)

A link is an active word or picture on a webpage that lets you go to another webpage or website by clicking on it. Links are usually a different colour or underlined and when you move your cursor on to one it will change into a hand (just to make life easier for you).

Modem

A modem is a device that allows your computer to talk to other computers. They do this by turning all of the information going to and from a computer into small pieces of digital sound and sending it through normal telephone lines to other computers.

MP3 (Motion Picture Experts Group audio layer 3)

A computer file format designed to store music in one twelfth of the space of CDs, for faster downloading and easy storage.

Online

Another way of saying that you are currently connected to the internet.

Off-line

Another way of saying you are not currently connected to the internet.

Plug-in

A small piece of software that adds features or functions to
your existing computer software. Plug-ins enable browsers to
play audio and video and the good thing is, once you've
downloaded them, they automatically install themselves – so
you don't have to!

Search engine

A specialist website which allows you to look for information on
the web either by categories or typing keywords into a little
box.

Server

A server is a large computer that holds information and
programmes for the internet. All servers use HTML to
communicate with each other so people can access the
information that they store.

Shareware

Software that you can download from the net for free to try out.
If you like it and use it you're meant to send payment to the
author.

Software

Computer programmes that instruct
your 'puter on what to do whether it's
to browse the internet, use a word
processing application or play a game.
Most software is already installed on
to your computer, but you can either
buy or download new software from
the internet to add to the things that
your computer can already do.

Surfing

Looking for sites on the internet in a random kinda way.

Upload

Uploading means to transfer words or pictures from your computer on to another computer, either via e-mail or directly on to the internet as a webpage or a website.

URL (Uniform Resource Locator)

Needlessly complicated expression for a website address.

Virus

A virus is a programme which harms the information inside your computer and can even stop it working. Viruses can be passed on via e-mail and when opened destroy your computer software. You can install anti-virus programmes which will detect these pesky viruses and, quite literally, kill 'em!

WAP [Wireless Application Protocol]

Nifty digital communications system that lets you access the internet and read your e-mails from the keypad of your mobile phone.

Website

A website is a collection of pages that are usually connected to one company, organization or person.

World wide web (www)

Also known as the internet.

Quiz

The fun bit at the end

Congratulations!
You've reached the end of this book with your sanity intact. By now you're e-mailing, chatting and designing websites like there's no tomorrow.

Before you go, try this techie quiz. Don't worry if you haven't done all the stuff in the previous chapters - just choose the answer that you feel most drawn to.

Are you a techno geek or a techno freak

1 What's your ideal e-mail name?

a) geekgirl@gurlpages.com

b) marsbareater@gurlpages.com

c) janesmith@gurlpages.com

2 **Someone's bombarding you with emoticons in a chat-room. Can you cope?**

a) Sure you can cope. You bombard them with emoticons, including some clever little codes that you cooked up specially for the occasion.

b) You can just about decipher most of them with the help of your emoticon dictionary, but in the end you tell 'em to learn to type properly.

c) Yikes! You get all flustered and log out of the chat-room before your head explodes.

3 **Your computer crashes - how do you deal?**

a) Hey, your computer never crashes, it wouldn't dare. And besides you always back up everything. Twice.

b) You say a quick prayer to the goddess of the hard disk and pray you haven't lost anything as you prepare to reboot your stoopid computer.

c) You yell hysterically for your 'rents to come to your aid, before bursting into tears.

4 **Downloads, discuss.**

a) You're the download queen. In fact, you've downloaded so much stuff you had to install a new hard drive which took you, ooh, all of five minutes.

b) You've just about got the hang of down loading stuff, but sometimes it gets a bit dicey.

c) You wouldn't know what a download was if it bit you on the nose.

5 **If you had a website what would it be about?**

a) Actually you've already got five websites. One for your favourite techie tips and freeware you've coded. One which works as an advice centre for net queries and one...

b) Funnily enough you've been thinking about creating a website and it's probably going to be about chocolate and your dog, Snuffles.

c) Website? Ha! It's all you can do to keep a diary.

6 **How many websites have you got book marked?**

a) 763 at the last count.

b) About twenty-five, but you're always forgetting to bookmark websites and then spend hours the next day trying to find them again.

c) Bookmarks? Aren't they for putting in erm, books?

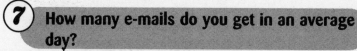

7 **How many e-mails do you get in an average day?**

a) Well you've got five different e-mail accounts so they tend to mount up. Upwards of fifty on a quiet day you reckon.

b) About five a day but that doesn't include the twenty text messages.

c) You're still getting round to sorting out an e-mail account.

8 **How do you stop your 'rents nagging at you for hogging the phone line?**

a) They've given up moaning at you and got you your own phone line for Christmas.

b) By having a full-blown hissy-fit as you pretend you're using the net for home work. Suckers!

c) Your 'rents would never nag at you for hogging the phone line 'cause, well, you don't.

How did you do?

Mostly As

Net Queen

You were probably born with a mouse in your hand. You rule the world wide web and there isn't a piece of computer software invented that would give you technical difficulties. In fact, you probably didn't even read this book - you probably wrote it!

Mostly Bs

Net Princess

Congratulations. You know your way round the internet, but like most of us you sometimes need a little bit of help when you get stuck. The cool thing about you is your willingness to learn new ways to work the web, so let us know when you get your website sorted out and we'll be surfing your way.

Mostly Cs

Net Phobic

Oh dear, oh dear, you just don't like all this new fangled computer talk, do you? Your biggest problem is your lack of confidence when it comes to connecting with the internet. But don't be put off, have another read of this book, take a deep breath and get online. You never know, you might like it!

Notes

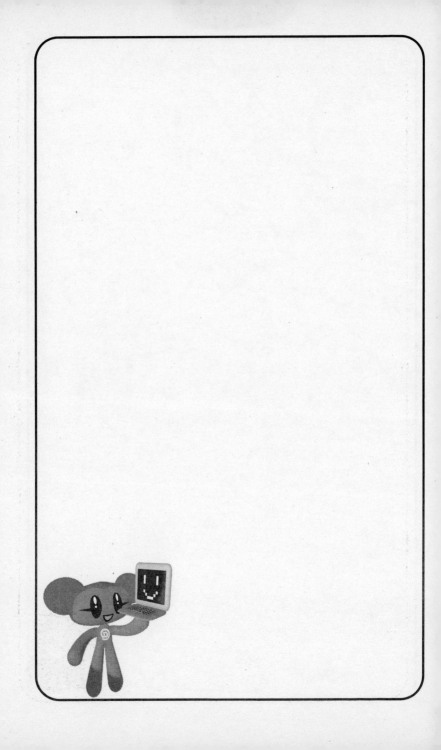

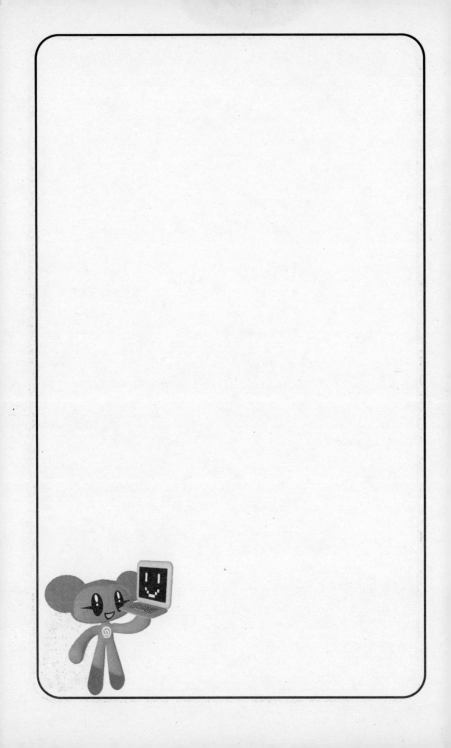

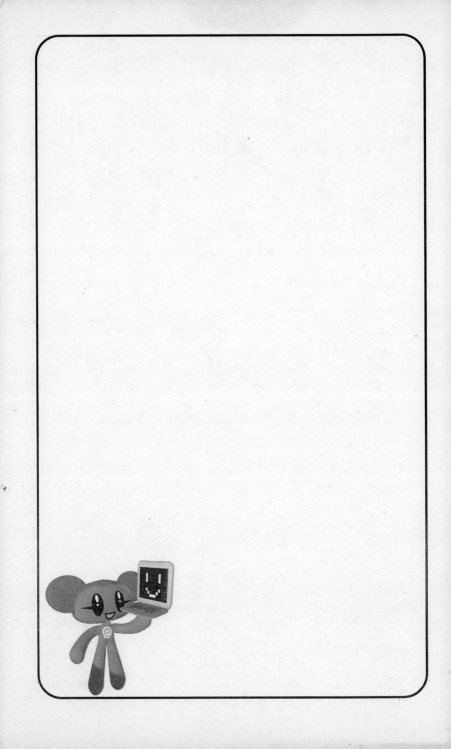